First World War
and Army of Occupation
War Diary
France, Belgium and Germany

2 DIVISION
19 Infantry Brigade,
Brigade Ammunition Column
21 August 1914 - 24 August 1915

WO95/1367/3

The Naval & Military Press Ltd
www.nmarchive.com
Published in association with The National Archives

Published by

The Naval & Military Press Ltd

Unit 10 Ridgewood Industrial Park,

Uckfield, East Sussex,

TN22 5QE England

Tel: +44 (0) 1825 749494

www.naval-military-press.com

www.nmarchive.com

This diary has been reprinted in facsimile from the original. Any imperfections are inevitably reproduced and the quality may fall short of modern type and cartographic standards.

© **Crown Copyright**
Images reproduced by permission of The National Archives, London, England, 2015.

Contents

Document type	Place/Title	Date From	Date To
Heading	WO95/1367 Bde Ammo Column		
Heading	2 Division 19 Bde Ammo Column 1914 Aug-1915 Aug		
Heading	19th Infantry Brigade. 19th Infantry Brigade Ammunition Column August 1914		
Heading	War Diary 19th Inf. Bde Ammunition Column From 21st August 1914 To 31st August K1914 (Volume 1)		
War Diary	Havre	21/08/1914	22/08/1914
War Diary	Valenciens	23/08/1914	24/08/1914
War Diary	Jenlain	25/08/1914	25/08/1914
War Diary	Le Cateau	26/08/1914	26/08/1914
War Diary	Noyon	27/08/1914	27/08/1914
War Diary	Pontoise	28/08/1914	29/08/1914
War Diary	Couloisy	30/08/1914	31/08/1914
War Diary	St Quentin	26/08/1914	26/08/1914
Heading	Noyon	27/08/1914	27/08/1914
Heading	19th Infantry Brigade. 19th Infantry Brigade Ammunition Column September 1914		
Heading	War Diary of 19th Inf Brigade Ammunition Column From 1st Sept To 30th Sept 1915 (Volume II)		
War Diary	Saintines	01/09/1914	01/09/1914
War Diary	War Diary of 19th Inf Bde Ammunition Column.	02/09/1914	02/09/1914
War Diary	Dammartin	02/09/1914	02/09/1914
War Diary	Lagny	03/09/1914	04/09/1914
War Diary	Brie-Comte Robert	05/09/1914	05/09/1914
War Diary	Grisy	06/09/1914	06/09/1914
War Diary	Alleneuve St Denis	07/09/1914	07/09/1914
War Diary	La Haute Maison	08/09/1914	08/09/1914
War Diary	Signy Signets	09/09/1914	10/09/1914
War Diary	Certigny	11/09/1914	11/09/1914
War Diary	Passy In Valois	12/09/1914	12/09/1914
War Diary	Buzancy	13/09/1914	13/09/1914
War Diary	Septmonts	14/09/1914	14/09/1914
War Diary	Venizel	14/09/1914	20/09/1914
War Diary	Septmonts	21/09/1914	30/09/1914
Heading	19th Infantry Brigade. 19th Brigade Ammunition Column October 1914		
Heading	War Diary of 19th Infantry Brigade Ammunition Column From 1st October 1914 To 31st October 1914 Volume III		
War Diary	Septmonts	01/10/1914	05/10/1914
War Diary	St Remy	06/10/1914	06/10/1914
War Diary	Vez	07/10/1914	07/10/1914
War Diary	Bethisy St Pierre	08/10/1914	08/10/1914
War Diary	Pont St Mayence	09/10/1914	10/10/1914
War Diary	St Omer	11/10/1914	11/10/1914
War Diary	Renescure	12/10/1914	12/10/1914
War Diary	Borre	13/10/1914	14/10/1914
War Diary	Baizieux	15/10/1914	15/10/1914
War Diary	Steenwerke	16/10/1914	16/10/1914
War Diary	Vlamertinge	17/10/1914	19/10/1914

War Diary	Laventie	20/10/1914	21/10/1914
War Diary	Croix Blanche	21/10/1914	26/10/1914
War Diary	Rue Du Quesnes X Rd	27/10/1914	31/10/1914
Heading	19th Infantry Brigade. 19th Infantry Brigade Ammunition Column November 1914		
Heading	War Diary of 19th Infantry Brigade Ammunition Column From 1st Nov 1914 To 30th Nov 1914 Volume IV		
War Diary	Rue Du Quesnes X Rd	01/11/1914	12/11/1914
War Diary	Rue Bataille	13/11/1914	17/11/1914
War Diary	Armentieres	18/11/1914	30/11/1914
Heading	19th Infantry Brigade Ammunition Column A December 1914		
Heading	6th Div. War Diary of 19th Infantry Brigade Ammunition Column From 1st Dec 1914 To 31st Dec 1914 Volume V		
War Diary	Armentieres	01/12/1914	31/12/1914
Heading	War Diary of 19th Infantry Brigade Ammunition Column From 1st January 1915 To 31st January 1915 Volume VI		
War Diary	Armentieres	01/01/1915	02/01/1915
War Diary	Rue Des Acquets	03/01/1915	31/01/1915
Heading	War Diary of 19th Infantry Bde. Ammunition Column From 1st February 1915 To 28th February 1915 Volume VII		
War Diary	Rue Des Acquets	01/02/1915	28/02/1915
Heading	19th Bde Ammn Coln Vol VIII 1-31.3.15		
Heading	War Diary of 19th Infantry Brigade Ammunition Column From March 1st 1915 To March 31st 1915 Volume VIII		
War Diary	(Erquingem) Rue Des Acquets	01/03/1915	11/03/1915
War Diary	Rue Des Acquets	12/03/1915	31/03/1915
Heading	War Diary of 19th Infantry Brigade Ammunition Column From 1st April 1915 To 30th April 1915 Volume IX		
War Diary	(Erquingem) Rue Des Acquets	01/04/1915	07/04/1915
War Diary	Rue Des Acquets	08/04/1915	30/04/1915
Heading	19th Brigade Ammn Coln Vol X 1-31.5.15		
Heading	War Diary of 19th Infantry Brigade Ammunition Column From 1st May 1915 To 31st May 1915 Volume X		
War Diary	Erquinghem Rue Des Acquets	01/05/1915	06/05/1915
War Diary	Rue Des Acquets	07/05/1915	31/05/1915
Heading	27th Division 19th Infy Bde 19th Bde Ammn Column Jun-Aug 1915		
Heading	27th Division. War Diary. 19th Infantry Brigade Ammunition Column. June 1915		
Heading	War Diary of 19th Infantry Brigade Ammunition Column From 1st June 1915 To 30th June 1915 Volume XI		
War Diary	Erquinghem Rue Des Acquets	01/06/1915	09/06/1915
War Diary	Rue Des Acquets	10/06/1915	30/06/1915
Heading	27th Division War Diary. 19th Infantry Brigade Ammunition Column July 1915		
Heading	War Diary of Ammunition Column 19th Infantry Brigade From 1-7-15 To 31-7-15 Volume XII		

War Diary	Erquinghem Rue Des Acquets	01/07/1915	08/07/1915
War Diary	Rue Des Acquets	09/07/1915	23/07/1915
War Diary	Le Nouveau Monde	24/07/1915	29/07/1915
War Diary	Nouveau Monde	30/07/1915	31/07/1915
Heading	27th Division. (Unit ceased 24.8.15) War Diary 19th Infantry Brigade Ammunition Column. August 1st To 24th 1915		
Heading	War Diary of 19th Infantry Brigade Ammunition Column From 1st August 24 Aug 1915 Volume XII		
War Diary	Nouveau Monde	01/08/1915	08/08/1915
War Diary	Le Nouveau Monde	09/08/1915	14/08/1915
War Diary	Nouveau Monde	15/08/1915	21/08/1915
War Diary	Therouanne	22/08/1915	22/08/1915
War Diary	Fressin	23/08/1915	23/08/1915
War Diary	Le Boisle	24/08/1915	24/08/1915

W0951367
Kate Cumming Collins

2 DIVISION

19 BDE

BDE AMMO COLUMN

1914 AUG - 1915 AUG

19th Infantry Brigade.

19th INFANTRY BRIGADE AMMUNITION COLUMN

AUGUST 1914.

CONFIDENTIAL

War Diary
of
19th Inf. Bde Ammunition
Column

from 21st August to 31st August
1914   1914

(Volume I)

2nd Lt W. BRIAN FROOK
mobilized with 5th Reserve Park
A.S.C and remained with them till
sent with 16 wagons and
18 men to HANGAR au COTONS
HAVRE where we were
mobilized into 19th Inf. Bde
Ammunition Column.

HAVRE
Aug. 21st
11 pm
Drew 600 boxes of S.A.A.
Remained all night at
HANGAR AU COTONS

HAVRE
Aug 22nd
Was told to entrain as 19th
Bde Ammunition Column
at Point 4. at 1.15 pm
Given 31 men 1 Cpl details
from 35, 31 and 28 coys
A.S.C to complete est. WBF.
Drew 4 days rations and entrained.

VALENCIENS
Aug 23rd
Arrived here 11 A.M and
was joined by Sergt JAMES
and 16 men 1st Middlesex
Regt as permanent escort.
A Platoon of Argyll and Suth.
Highlanders met us and
escorted us to LES ECOLES,
VALENCIENS.
5 pm Marched to join 19th Inf Bde

at BLANC MISSERON, where I reported to GENERAL DRUMMOND comdg 19th Bde at 11 p.m.

Aug 24th
1 AM
marched out with the Brigade Train and waited on the ETOUGES Rd during the Battle of MONS returning through ROISIN, VILLERSPOL to PRESAV, where we moved with the brigade to JENLAIN arriving there at 7 p.m. Billeted.

JENLAIN
Aug 25th
3 AM
marched towards SOLESMES Fired on by party of Uhlans no one hit! Received orders to remain at X rds N of SOLESMES till ordered to move. 4 p.m. moved to LE CATEAU where we bivouaced 9 pm

LE CATEAU
Aug 26th
3.30 AM
moved in rear of Train to MARETZ where we halted while the supply wagons completed refilling. 10 AM moved on to ESTREES where we halted at about 1.30 p.m. Rumour of defeat

7

and GERMAN advance on ESTREES moved with Brigade train and other details of Trains and Ammunition Columns towards ST QUENTIN, arriving about 8 p.m. When preparing to billet were suddenly told ~~we were to~~ that the brigade was cut up and we were to be entrained to NOYON left ST QUENTIN at 11.30 p.m. Germans expected hourly. ↑ with Brigade Train and escort of Argyll and Sutherland Highlanders and numerous other details of transport.

yes
See Appendix I

NOYON
Aug 27
1 p.m.

Reached a point ½ mile N. of NOYON. Apparently reports of previous night erroneous; as we were ordered to bivouac here by a Staff Officer. Remained here till 4 p.m. Our first rest for horses ~~since~~ to be unhooked since 3.30 A.M. Aug 26th.

WHS

NOYON Aug 27ᵗʰ (Contd.)	At 3 p.m moved on to NOYON where the Ammunition Column was bivouaced in the CAVALRY BARRACKS for the night, a rest much needed by men and horses. WHJ
Aug 28ᵗʰ PONTOISE	Moved here from NOYON at 9 AM where the day and night were spent. It was anticipated a 3 days rest was to be spent here but on WHJ
PONTOISE Aug 29ᵗʰ 6 p.m.	the following day the brigade moved on a long march commencing at 6 pm. to COULOISY. the army still being in retreat. Another rest was anticipated here but owing to the very rapid advance of the enemy orders were received to move with the train on a march towards VERBERIE reaching SAINTINES at 9 p.m. Bivouaced. Germans were pressing our retreat allowing the troops little rest.
COULOISY Aug 30ᵗʰ 5 p.m.	
Aug 31ˢᵗ 5.45 am	

WHJ

APPENDIX I

ST QUENTIN
Aug 26th
11 p.m.

After the order was received to proceed to NOYON the AMMUNITION COLUMN was ordered to march in rear of the 19th Inf Bde baggage train. The confusion at the starting point, the market square in ST QUENTIN, was such that the various units of the convoy, which included ambulance wagons, motor lorries and details of Div Train, were split up. During the march an order was passed down from the head of the column to lighten the loads. The escort and drivers proceeded to discard a great quantity of stores the nature of which it was impossible to ascertain in the dark.
WBF

NOYON
Aug 27th
1 p.m.

On reaching here the Ammunition Col was found to be deficient of 431 boxes of S.A.A. (out of an est. of 600 boxes), several mens kits and one officers valise complete.
2Lt W. BRIAN FROOK reported loss to 19th Inf Bde Headquarters on Aug 28th
WBF

19th Infantry Brigade.

19th INFANTRY BRIGADE AMMUNITION COLUMN

SEPTEMBER 1914.

A.2

CONFIDENTIAL.

121/1084

WAR DIARY
of
19th Inf. Brigade Ammunition Column

from 1st Sept — to 30th Sept
1914   1914

(VOLUME II)

seen by A.2.

WAR DIARY
of
19th Inf. Bde. Ammunition Column.

Hour Date Place	Summary of Events.	Reference Remarks
SAINTINES 1st Sept 3 AM	Orders received to join the 4th Divisional Train, and proceed with them to BARON. Heavy mist, & saved the train from being shelled when crossing within range of enemy's guns. All spare men and escort used to protect left flank. Good order was maintained throughout the march.	WTJS
BARON 2nd Sept 12 noon	Reached BARON at noon. Horses very fatigued. Parked in road side. Several alarms that German cavalry were entering the town. Here 19th Inf Bde joined us about 6 p.m. bringing 60 prisoners and 3 guns.	
12 midnight	Ordered to proceed with Bde Train in rear of 4th Div. Train. Destination unknown.	WTJS

		12

DAMMARTIN
Sept 2nd
9 AM

Arrived here at 9 AM and bivouaced. Troops came in all day 4th Division.

10.30 pm

Orders received to move off Ammunition Column being in front of the Brigade train followed by 4th Divisional train. Cavalry ⊕ Clearing the front as German Cavalry was reputed to be endeavouring to intercept the convoy. marched all night VIA JUILLY — CLAYE-SOUILLY — ANNET to LAGNY   WHF

LAGNY
Sept 3rd
8 AM

Arrived here after a very long uninterrupted march at 8 AM Bivouaced just South of LAGNY on the outskirts of the town 4th Divisional Train being with the 19th Bde Train and Amm. Column. Remained here all the 3rd and night of 4th Sept.   WHF

LAGNY
Sept 4th
10 pm

Continued the march in a S.W. direction. no destination being known to 2/Lt FLOOK I/c Ammunition Column

BRIE-COMTE ROBERT 7 AM. Sept 5th	Arrived here after heavy march. Route unknown. Halted for 2 hours here during which refilled 321 boxes of S.A.A. from 19th Inf. Bde. Ammunition Park it being en route for own Railhead VILLENEUVE-ST-GEORGES. Load of Ammunition carried now 500 boxes; verbal permission being obtained here from headquarters to reduce est. from 600 boxes to 500 to allow for a supply waggon and lighter loads.
9 AM	Proceeded with 19th Brigade to GRISY. Bivouaced in MARKET SQUARE. This was last place of retirement.
GRISY Sept 6th	Brigadier-General HON. F. GORDON assumed command of 19th Inf Bde. (writ)
5 AM	Left GRISY with 19th Inf Bde Ammunition Column now marching with Brigade in rear of last battalion and in front of 19th Field Ambulance. Marched to

	VILLENEUVE-ST-DENIS arriving 6 pm; Bivouaced the night. This march was the first advance made by the 19th Inf. Brigade. 4th Division in touch with enemy's rearguard to our front.
VILLENEUVE ST-DENIS Sept 7th 9·30 AM	Marched with Brigade (after drawing supplies from train) to a point S.W. of LA HAUTE MAISON. Bivouaced. W3½
LA-HAUTE MAISON Sept 8th 3 AM	Marched via LA-HAUTE MAISON — PIERRE-LEVEE to a point 1½ miles from SIGNY-SIGNETS, where 1st MIDDLESEX Regt leading the Brigade was shelled by shrapnel from enemy's guns on a ridge the other side of the valley. 1st line Transport, Ammunition Column and Field Ambulance halted on roadside for 3 hours while infantry went into action.
5 AM	
9 AM	Enemy's guns retired. Road reported clear. Marched down the hill into the valley and bivouaced in a hollow just S.E.

15

of SIGNY-SIGNETS. 19th Inf. Bde
now participating in the BATTLE
of the MARNE.   WBF

SIGNY-SIGNETS
Sept 9th
7.30AM
 Enemy's guns at this hour began
to drop shrapnel near the
bivouac and also the bivouac
of the 19th Field Ambulance on
our right. 2/Lt F TOOK moved
the Ammunition Column to a
more sheltered spot on the
road 300 yds back; shrapnel
bullets striking the rear
wagon, but causing no
casualties.

3 PM Enemy's guns silenced.
Ammunition Column returned
to its bivouac and remained
there.   WBF

SIGNY-SIGNETS
Sept 10th
4 AM.
 marched with 19th Brigade
via JOUARRE and crossed pontoon
bridge (bridge being destroyed)
at LA FERTE-SOUS-JOUARRE at
11AM and proceeded via LA
RUE bivouacing the night
at CERTIGNY. The 19th Brigade
forming left flank guard
to 3rd Army Corps.   WBF

CERTIGNY Sept 11th 8 AM	Advanced with Brigade via VAUX-SOUS-COULOMBS to CERFROID where Ammunition Column was ordered to park with 4th Div. Ammunition Column already there. Remained here till 3 pm when it marched in rear of 4th Div. Amm. Col. via ST QUENTIN till within a mile of PASSY-en-VALOIS where owing heavy going several wagons stuck. Much was lost with the 4th Div. Amm. Cols. as their 6 horsed limbers were more easily drawn than the 2 horsed A.S.C. wagons. Bivouaced on road side 11 pm
PASSY-en-VALOIS Sept 12 5 AM	Moved through PASSY la VALOIS to MARIZY-STE-GENEVIEVE where 19th Bde Train was parked. Brigade having moved with 4th Division towards CHOUY. Ammunition Column moved via MARIZY-ST-MARD to CHOUY (to avoid congestion) and took its place on line of

march behind 19th Field Ambulance and continued with Brigade via VILLERS-HELON — VILLEMONTOIRE to BUZANCY which was reached in torrents of rain at 9 p.m. Wagons and horses had to be left parked. Men billeted.

BUZANCY
Sept. 13th
1.30 p.m.

Remained here till 1.30 p.m. when the Column marched with the Brigade to SEPTMONTS where a halt was made by roadside till 3 A.M.

SEPTMONTS
Sept 14
3 A.M.

when the Brigade marched via BILLY-SUR-AISNE to X rds ½ mile N of C. in le CARRIER (Ref map sheet 33 SOISSONS N.E.) where it bivouacked.

VENIZEL
Sept 14
5 am

O.C. Ammunition Column was ordered to leave 8 wagons at SEPTMONTS which he did under Scout JAMES and proceed with Brigade with other 8 wagons. Parked near 19th Field Ambulance behind a ledge ¼ mile from

Bde. Headquarters on main road.

9 AM — Discovered by enemy's heavy artillery; shelled at intervals all day. Horses and men were moved up into woods with 19th Field Amb. Horses and men no casualties occurred but one ammunition wagon was hit and rear wheel blown off. Bandolier at rear of wagon exploded, but no boxes of SAA were damaged.

7 pm — After dark horses were hooked in to 7 wagons, and orders were received to proceed near headquarters. Impossible to move damaged wagon in dark but unloaded it.

WBF

VENIZEL
Sept 15th
5 AM — Returned for damaged wagon, repaired wheel and brought it in. Battle of AISNE in progress. 19th Inf Bde bivouacked in woods in reserve.

WBF

VENIZEL
Sept 16th
9 AM — 2Lt F. took rode back to SEPTMONTS to meet O.C. 19th Bde Amm.

Park. 40 boxes SAA drawn and loaded in Ammunition Column wagons at SEPTMONTS (those at VENIZEL fully loaded). MOTOR returned to VENIZEL. W/F

VENIZEL
Sept 17th
Nothing of note with reference to Ammunition Column occurred. Pay drawn for men. W/F

VENIZEL
Sept 18th
No change of position of 19th Inf Bde. W/F

VENIZEL
Sept 19th
Men at VENIZEL paid out. The remaining half at SEPTMONTS also paid out. No change in position. W/F

VENIZEL
Sept 20th
11 AM
Orders received that Brigade would move after dark to SEPTMONTS. 1 NCO sent to join billeting party.
8 pm marched to SEPTMONTS Wagons parked in field next to 14th Field Ambulance. Billeted in Factory with men of Field Ambulance. W/F

SEPTMONTS
Sept 21st
Nothing of note occurred. Standing orders issued. W/F

SEPTMONTS
Sept 22nd — Fine and Sunny. Veterinary Insp of horses. 8. Remount Heavy Draught horses received. 5 horses returned unfit. Numbers now complete 1½ spare pair. Harness thoroughly cleaned. Rifle inspection. WSH

SEPTMONTS
Sept 23rd — Fine and Sunny.
Nothing of note occurred. Horses exercised. Rifle inspection. Wagons inspected and greased. WSH

SEPTMONTS
Sept 24th — Fine and Sunny.
Issued 7000 rounds S.A.A. to Argyll and Sutherland Highlanders. Usual parades held. WSH

SEPTMONTS
Sept 25th — Fine and Sunny, Colder.
Issued 2000 rounds SAA to 1st Middlesex Regt. and 12200 rounds to Argyll and Suth. Highlanders. Usual Parades held. WSH

SEPTMONTS Sept 26th	Fine but must colder. Issued 7000 rounds S.A.A. to Arg. & Sueth. Highlanders and 300 rounds revolver ammunition to 1st Cameronians, 72 rounds to Headquarters 19th Inf. Bde. Usual parades held
SEPTMONTS Sept 27th	Sunday. Fine and a little warmer. Church Parade held at 10 A.M. At 6 A.M. orders received to be ready to move off as soon as Reserve Ammunition Column ready to move at 6.45 a.m. horses being watered and fed. 7.0 A.M. orders cancelled.
7.15 p.m.	Orders received that 19th Inf. Bde. would, till further orders, be ready to move by 5 A.M. daily
SEPTMONTS Sept 28th	4 A.M. Reveille. Fine but cold. Brigade ready to move 5 A.M. — 6 A.M. orders to fall out. Issued 5000 to Argyll and

Sutherland Highlanders.
Drew 39,000 rounds S.A.A and
1800 rounds revolver
ammunition from 5th Div
Ammunition Park.
Usual Parades held. WHJ

SEPT MONTH
Sept 29th

Reveille 4 A.M. Stood ready to
move till orders received to
dismiss 6 A.M. Fine and Cold

10 A.M Ammunition Column was
visited and inspected by
Brigadier-General J.D. GILPIN
A.D. of S.T. who expressed
himself satisfied with the
condition of the horses and
routine of the Column.

12 noon Horses inspected by P.V.O.
3rd Army Corps. who also
expressed satisfaction at
condition of horses.
Issued 368 rounds revolver
ammunition to R. Welsh Fusiliers. WHJ

SEPT MONTH
Sept 30th

Reveille 4 A.M. Dismissed 6 A.M.
Fine and Cold. Issued
456,000 rounds S.A.A to Argyll
& Sutherland Highlanders.

End of Vol II   WHJ

19th Infantry Brigade.

19th BRIGADE AMMUNITION COLUMN

OCTOBER 1914.

A2

WAR DIARY
of
19th INFANTRY BRIGADE
AMMUNITION COLUMN

From 1st October 1914 — to 31st October 1914 inclusive

VOLUME III

Army Form C. 2118.

WAR DIARY
or
INTELLIGENCE SUMMARY.
(Erase heading not required.)

Instructions regarding War Diaries and Intelligence Summaries are contained in F.S. Regs., Part II. and the Staff Manual respectively. Title pages will be prepared in manuscript.

Hour, Date, Place		Summary of Events and Information	Remarks and references to Appendices
SEPTMONTS. 1st Oct 1914.	5 AM	Paraded ready to move on arrival.	
	11 AM	Received S.A.A. from 5th Div. Park and completed ammunition.	
	10 AM	15th Fd. Bde. Ammunition Column was inspected by Brig-General F. GORDON commanding 19th Brigade	
SEPTMONTS 2nd Oct.	8 AM	Paraded ready to move as usual. Nothing of importance occurred. Firm but held day.	
SEPTMONTS 3rd Oct	8 AM	Paraded ready to move. Being Sunday church parade was held at 10 AM.	
SEPTMONTS 4th Oct.	8 AM	Paraded ready to move as usual. 2nd Floor received orders to attend at Hd Quarters at 10.30 AM where he was told to prepare to move that night.	
	7.30 pm	Moved with Brigade VIA EQUIRY – CHACRISE to St. REMY where we bivouaced at 4 AM	
SEPTMONTS 5th Oct			
St REMY 6 Oct		Remained here all day. Issued 4000 rds S.A.A. to Argyll & Sutherlands, and drew same from 5th Div. Park. Continued march via NADON-FE – CORCY – FLEURY	
	7.30 pm		

Army Form C. 2118.

WAR DIARY
or
INTELLIGENCE SUMMARY.
(Erase heading not required.)

Instructions regarding War Diaries and Intelligence Summaries are contained in F.S. Regs., Part II. and the Staff Manual respectively. Title pages will be prepared in manuscript.

Hour, Date, Place	Summary of Events and Information	Remarks and references to Appendices
VEZ 7 Oct. 9.30 AM	— VILLERS – COTTERÊTS – LARGNY & VEZ. Arrived at VEZ when being dispersed from billets overflown by enemy aircraft at 6.30 pm entered the march via Orrouy to BETHISY – ST – PIERRE arriving 12.30 AM. Bivouacked.	
BETHISY-ST-PIERRE 8 Oct 2p	Brigade marched in two columns, Brunetière between marked with left column via RHUIS & PONT-ST-MAXENCE when left column was to actual movements being cancelled columns bivouaced there.	
PONT-ST-MAXENCE 9 Oct 7.30AM	Proceeded with left column via CLINCOURT to ESTRÉES-ST-DENIS. Bivouaced at 12.30 pm and right column of Brigade arrived about 11.30 pm. Entrainment commenced 4 pm, 2 wagon and 12 horses of ammunition column entrained in 2nd train at 8 pm under Cpl. KNIGHTS A.S.C. Remainder 14 wagons 30 horses entrained at 12 midnight	

Army Form C. 2118.

WAR DIARY
or
INTELLIGENCE SUMMARY.
(Erase heading not required.)

Instructions regarding War Diaries and Intelligence Summaries are contained in F.S. Regs., Part II. and the Staff Manual respectively. Title pages will be prepared in manuscript.

Hour, Date, Place	Summary of Events and Information	Remarks and references to Appendices
	under 2Lt W.O. FEDDIE a 3rd Draft. Party Arrived ETAPLES	
10th Oct 5pm	- BOULOGNE - CALAIS Arrived at a detraining point 5 miles from ST OMER. considerable difficulty was experienced in loading all wheeled G.S. wagons on to the French covered trucks. After a considerable delay the 3rd Draft under Col WARD 1st Middlesex proceeded to ST OMER where billets were already allotted. Arrived 11.30 pm.	
ST OMER 11th Oct 5:30 AM	Moved with brigade via ARQUES & RENESCURE. Billeted	
RENESCURE 12th Oct 9:15 AM	+50 min moved with brigade via EBBLINGHEM - LES CING RUES - to HAZEBROUCK where ammunition column was ordered to halt. Bivouaced 1.15 pm till 4.30 pm when it was ordered to proceed to BORRE. Billeted here.	
BORRE 13th Oct 7:30 AM	Ammunition column ordered to proceed to place of assembly of Brigade at ROUGE CROIX. Remained behind brigade just Nth BORRE - PRADELLES RD from 11 AM to 6 pm when orders were	

WAR DIARY
or
INTELLIGENCE SUMMARY.
(Erase heading not required.)

Army Form C. 2118.

Instructions regarding War Diaries and Intelligence
Summaries are contained in F.S. Regs., Part II.
and the Staff Manual respectively. Title pages
will be prepared in manuscript.

Hour, Date, Place	Summary of Events and Information	Remarks and references to Appendices
14 Oct		
11.30 AM	Received orders to remain in present position in readiness for the night. Relieved from duties.	
	Received orders to move to men to rouge Croix joined Brigade there and marched with them on STRAZEELE - MOUT ENASIER to BAILLEUR. Brigade halted here at S.W. - RUE de LILLE. Ammunition Column here - RUE des PUISONS. Organizations were made out transmission columns were inspected at 10.30 p.m. To billet when in was.	
BAILLEUL 15 Oct 7.0 p	Received orders to march in rear of Brigade via third crossing, 1 mile S.W BAILLEUR to junction of 5 roads S.W. of STEENWERKE. Bivouacked in field here.	
W STEENWERKE 16 Oct 12.30 p	Moved with brigade via STEENWERKE - NEUVE EGLISE - KEMMEL - LA CLYTTE - POUCE - OUDERDOM VLAMERTINCHE which was reached at 10 p.m. after a long march. Billeted.	
YLAMERTINGE 17 Oct	Remained in billets here on reserve brigade to 5th Divi.	
" 18 Oct	Remained here today. Still in reserve.	

(9 29 6) W 2794 100,000 8/14 H W V Forms/C. 2118/11.

WAR DIARY
or
INTELLIGENCE SUMMARY
(Erase heading not required.)

Army Form C. 2118.

Hour, Date, Place	Summary of Events and Information	Remarks and references to Appendices

VLAMERTINGE 19th Oct. 11.30 Moved with brigade at about noon via OUDERDOM - Pont 6 - LA CLYTTE - KEMMET - NEUVE-EGLISE - STEENWERKE - ESTAIRES to LAVENTIE to join 3rd Army Corps.

LAVENTIE 20th Oct. 5 AM Arrived here after a very long march. Billeted.

12.30 pm Brigade mounted, set out to take up a position. Ammunition column remaining in billets to await orders.

LAVENTIE 21st Oct. 8 AM Received orders to proceed to CROIX BLANCHE and await. Parked in a lane. Billeted. Got in touch with 6th Divisional Amm. Column at SAILLY and Parks at ESTAIRES. Which were manned by 6th Div, Hd Qu. & 19th Bde Amm. Col B refile from 6th Div Amm Col, not Park owing to the distance at which army was. Moved 16 wd 10.35 pm. Heavy night attack on Brigade commenced about 9 PM. No horses

CROIX BLANCHE 5.30

WAR DIARY
or
INTELLIGENCE SUMMARY.
(Erase heading not required.)

Army Form C. 2118.

Instructions regarding War Diaries and Intelligence Summaries are contained in F.S. Regs., Part II. and the Staff Manual respectively. Title pages will be prepared in manuscript.

Hour, Date, Place	Summary of Events and Information	Remarks and references to Appendices
CROIX BLANCHE 21st Oct	were handed up in accordance with orders. Brigade fell back a little during the night, but not opposed to any extent a move by Ammunition Column.	
8.30 AM	Received orders to and E from wagons and personnel at CROIX MARÉCHAT and and to form a Brigade reserve of Ammunition with S.A.A. replenished cart. Arms 100 and and S.A.A. from 6th and A.C. Two advanced wagons were meanwhile unfilled, and 127 and and drawn. Total amount issued 160 and and S.A.A.	
CROIX BLANCHE 22nd Oct	6,000 rounds S.A.A. drawn. 2/Lt F.Scoll went to Brigade H.Q. quarters with reference to the proposed scheme for collecting the surplus ammunition dumped in the trenches, and obtained permission from the Brigadier-General that F GORDON to keep a reserve of 30,000 rounds instead of 5,000 so that if an extreme emergency with the Ammunition Column could pick up that surplus	

WAR DIARY
or
INTELLIGENCE SUMMARY.
(Erase heading not required.)

Army Form C. 2118.

Hour, Date, Place	Summary of Events and Information	Remarks and references to Appendices
CROIX BLANCHE 24th Oct	(roughly estimated at 2,000 our rounds); 64,000 rounds were issued to-day.	
	Drawing of ammunition for trenches and extra rounds per man continued, at dawn and dusk. 320,000 rounds were issued by E.P.M. About 9 pm a very heavy attack was made on 19th Infantry Brigade. Ammunition Column was almost nearly to move in relieved till attacks had been repulsed.	
CROIX BLANCHE 25th Oct 4.10 AM	264,000 rounds SAA were drawn at SAILLY. Instructions received at 6 pm from Brigade Hd Qrs to prepare for issue of a large amount of S.A.A. 100,000 more rounds were thereupon drawn and C. in C., and Park numbered 80,000 rounds only were however issued.	
CROIX BLANCHE 26th Oct 5 AM	Received orders to go back half a mile to RUE DU QUESNES cross roads. 70,000 rounds were issued to-day. The few rounds returned was examined ? then arrival there	

WAR DIARY
or
INTELLIGENCE SUMMARY

(Erase heading not required.)

Army Form C. 2118.

Instructions regarding War Diaries and Intelligence Summaries are contained in F.S. Regs., Part II. and the Staff Manual respectively. Title pages will be prepared in manuscript.

Hour, Date, Place	Summary of Events and Information	Remarks and references to Appendices
RUE DU QUESNES. Rd 27th Oct.	Our casualties (wounded) occurring to-day amongst the personnel were drawn to-day from Sutler of 6th Div	
	60,000 rounds were drawn to-day from Sutler of 6th Div	
	A.C. & RAE ST MAUR	
QUE.DU QUESNES. Rd 28th Oct.	60,000 rounds were drawn out 70,000 issued to-day	
RUE DU QUESNES. Rd 29th Oct.	2 AM. Good reserve to move during night to trenches. 100,000 rounds were issued during the early morning and some amount refilled.	
RUE DU QUESNES. Rd 30 Oct.	Issued 100,000 rds out and over the same amount. Belgian WHIR at 1000 percent events taken away in dribs in the trenches.	
RUE DU QUESNES. Rd 31st Oct.	80,000 rounds S.A.A. issued and 41,800 rounds drawn (850 lines)	
	End of VOLUME III	

19th Infantry Brigade.

19th INFANTRY BRIGADE AMMUNITION COLUMN

NOVEMBER 1914.

CONFIDENTIAL

WAR DIARY.
of
19th Infantry Brigade Ammunition Column

From 1st Nov. 1914 to 30th Nov. 1914.

VOLUME IV

121/2625

Army Form C. 2118

WAR DIARY
or
INTELLIGENCE SUMMARY.
(Erase heading not required.)

Instructions regarding War Diaries and Intelligence Summaries are contained in F.S. Regs., Part II. and the Staff Manual respectively. Title pages will be prepared in manuscript.

Hour, Date, Place	Summary of Events and Information	Remarks and references to Appendices
RUE DU QUESNES x Rd. 1st Nov. 1914	Found 32,000 rds S.A.A. Over 120,000 rds S.A.A. All wagon were thoroughly overhauled and wheels greased.	W.D. 5/
RUE DU QUESNES x Rd. 2nd Nov.	Issued 16,000 rds S.A.A. Arrangements were made to-day to collect the surplus ammunition in the trenches. The Brigade return to its second line by means of dumping 9 wagon loads and taking the empty wagons to the front line of trenches and carrying out carrying the surplus ammunition collected there to the second line of trenches.	
" 4th Nov.	Issued no ammunition. Quiet day.	W.D. 5/ W.D. 5/
" 5th Nov.	Issued no ammunition. Attack about 8 P.M. Signal Coy. No ammunition issued. 4 returned wagons were filled about 1pm. Horses and men had to be moved back under cover of some hay-stacks. No casualties.	
" 6th Nov.	Heavy fog. No S.A.A. issued.	W.D. 5/ W.D. 5/
" 7th Nov.	No ammunition issued.	W.D. 5/

(9 29 6) W 2794 100,000 8/14 H W V Forms/C. 2118/11.

Army Form C. 2118

WAR DIARY
or
INTELLIGENCE SUMMARY.
(Erase heading not required.)

Instructions regarding War Diaries and Intelligence Summaries are contained in F. S. Regs., Part II. and the Staff Manual respectively. Title pages will be prepared in manuscript.

Hour, Date, Place	Summary of Events and Information	Remarks and references to Appendices
RUE DU QUESNES × Rdg 8 Inf	Mild weather. Very quiet. No ammunition arrived. Arabs still haven't cleaned	
" 9th Nov	31000 rounds SAA issued today. 2 heavy draught horses received from Remount.	WRF
" 10 Nov	No ammunition issued. One heavy draught have returned to Det. Mobile Section	WRF
" 11 Nov	No ammunition issued. About 3 p.m. RUE DU QUESNES was shelled, 1st Fire being at Wilkes their home. Ammunition Column horses were also sent back. No casualties occurred, only 3 cows being killed. Received orders to move Column back.	WRF
" 12 Nov GHQ	Moved to road junction RUE BATAILLE and filled in a farm. The farm advanced waggon remained in their position.	WRF
RUE BATAILLE 13th Nov.	No ammunition issued. It was wet windy day	WRF
" 14th Nov	19th Infy Brigade were relieved tonight by 7 Division	WRF

(9 29 6) W 2791 100,000 8/14 H W V Forms/C. 2118/11.

WAR DIARY
or
INTELLIGENCE SUMMARY.
(Erase heading not required.)

Army Form C. 2118

Hour, Date, Place	Summary of Events and Information	Remarks and references to Appendices
	...went into billets in Rue St Maur and Smithy. Ammunition Column remained in its billet. Eye	
RUE ST MAILLE 15th Nov	KNIGHTS I/c & advanced wagon rejoined. Drew 26,000 rounds S.A.A. to complete units, as all machine gun ammunition in trenches had been handed over to relieving regiments.	W.B.T
16th	Issued 16,000 A/a to Gordon Highlanders who required ammunition urgently. Received intimation that Brigade would move the following day.	W.B.T
17 Nov	2nd afternoon advanced to Pradeel to Meerut & Rd Pont de NIEPPE to be shown and relieved billet by Staff Capt. 19 Ind Bde. Guards went at N.W. entrance to ARMENTIÈRES selected. Shed not quite ready to accommodate horses found good billets for all the horses of the unit.	
3.30 pm	marched via ERQUINGHEM to ARMENTIÈRES...	W.B.T

WAR DIARY
or
INTELLIGENCE SUMMARY.
(Erase heading not required.)

Army Form C. 2118

Hour, Date, Place	Summary of Events and Information	Remarks and references to Appendices
ARMENTIERES 18th Nov	4 wagons under Cpl. KNIGHTS who went to form with SAA regimental carts, the Brigade Ammunition Reserve at HOUPLINES.	W R F
19th Nov	At 6AM horses and personnel of 4 advanced wagons reported, with orders to return each evening at sundown between at dawn. 2 heavy draught ammunition received; also one from Brigade train for Supplies wagon.	W R F / W R F
20th Nov	32000 rds SAA issued to R.W. Fusiliers. No ammunition issued. All horses cleaned & clubbed.	
21st Nov	No SAA issued. V.I. inspection of horses Returned two to mobile section and one from Supply wagon train.	W R F
22nd Nov	Issued no ammunition. Rifle + harness inspection.	W R F
23rd Nov	Issued 16000 rds SAA to 5th Scottish Rifles, 64000 to Argyll + Sutherland, 32000 to 1st Middlesex.	W R F

WAR DIARY
or
INTELLIGENCE SUMMARY.
(Erase heading not required.)

Army Form C. 2118

Hour, Date, Place	Summary of Events and Information	Remarks and references to Appendices
ARMENTIERES 24th Nov.	Drew 120 000 rds SAA from 6th Div A.C. and 3 boxes of Revolver Ammunition	WPJ
" 25th Nov	Issued 6000 rds SAA & 1 box Revolver Ammunition	WPJ
"	Rifle inspection	WPJ
" 26th Nov.	No ammunition issued	WPJ
" 27th Nov	3000 rounds in red to 1st Middlesex	WPJ
" 28th Nov.	Issued 30 000 to Argyll & Sutherland Highlanders. Rifle inspection. Hammer dulcimised.	WPJ
" 29th Nov.	No ammunition issued.	WPJ
" 30th Nov.	Issued 10 000 rds to 5th Scottish Rifles	WPJ
	End of VOLUME IV	

19th Infantry Brigade

19th INFANTRY BRIGADE AMMUNITION COLUMN.

DECEMBER 1914.

CONFIDENTIAL.

6th Div.

WAR DIARY

of

19th Infantry Brigade Ammunition Column

From 1st Dec 1914 to 31st Dec 1914

VOLUME I

121/3909

Army Form C. 2118.

WAR DIARY
or
INTELLIGENCE SUMMARY.
(Erase heading not required.)

Instructions regarding War Diaries and Intelligence Summaries are contained in F.S. Regs., Part II. and the Staff Manual respectively. Title pages will be prepared in manuscript.

Hour, Date, Place	Summary of Events and Information	Remarks and references to Appendices
ARMENTIERES		
1914 1st Dec	No S.A.A. issued. 1,00000 rounds drawn from 6th Div.	W.P.T.
2nd Dec 9 PM	Collected 1500 boxes of S.A.A. issued from Hunter enquired to weather and rendered unfit for immediate use. This was cleared and handed over to 5th Scottish Rifles for practice. 10,000 rds of unexpended S.A.A. being received from them in exchange	W.P.T.
3rd Dec	No S.A.A. issued or drawn	W.P.T.
4th Dec	No S.A.A. issued or drawn. Harness cleaned and inspected	W.P.T.
5th Dec	No S.A.A. issued or drawn. 2Lt W.P.FROIS taken over from Lt R. BRODIE-MURRAY took command	W.P.T.
6th Dec	No S.A.A. issued or drawn. Rifles and Equipment Inspected	K.M.
7th Dec	Issue 2000 rounds to A & Y Highlanders. No S.A.A. drawn. Inspected Horses and Wagons	K.M.
8th Dec	No S.A.A. issued or drawn. Horse Inspection by O.C. Grooms and Veterinary Officer	K.M.

Army Form C. 2118

WAR DIARY
or
INTELLIGENCE SUMMARY
(Erase heading not required.)

Instructions regarding War Diaries and Intelligence Summaries are contained in F.S. Regs., Part II. and the Staff Manual respectively. Title pages will be prepared in manuscript.

Hour, Date, Place	Summary of Events and Information	Remarks and references to Appendices
ARMENTIERES 9th Dec 1914	No S.A.A. drawn. 1000 rounds Issued to A & S. Highlander. Two sacks of loose ammunition in chargers and bandoliers returned by A & S. Highlanders total 3500 rounds. This ammunition was in perfectly good condition and fit for use in Machine Guns.	KBR
10th Dec	Drawn from 6th Div. Ammunition Column 100,000 S.A.A. Issued to 1st Middx Regt. 48,000 rounds A & S. Highlander 48,000 rounds	KBR
11th Dec	Returned from Field Ambulance 4,500 rounds loose S.A.A. No S.A.A. drawn. Issued to 1st Middx Regt. 16,000 and to 1st Cameronians 19,000 rounds & 600 rounds (revolver) Returned from H.Q. 1000 rounds. 13 Boxes of loose ammunition (9000 rounds) returned to the 6th Div. Amm. Col. for repacking. Inspected Rifles, Horses & Saddles.	KBR
12th Dec	Drew 40,000 rounds S.A.A. 900 rounds Revolver. Issued to 1st Cameronians 16,000 rounds S.A.A. Inspected Rifles & Wagons.	KBR

WAR DIARY
INTELLIGENCE SUMMARY

Army Form C. 2118.

Hour, Date, Place	Summary of Events and Information	Remarks and references to Appendices
ARMENTIERES 13th Dec.	Drew 2160 rounds (Pointblank) to boxes (Empties) received from 5th Cameronians (Scottish Rifles) for return. No S.A.A. issued. Received 2 Bicycles for inter-communication purposes from D.O. Voluntary Church Parade at 11.45 A.M.	KBh
" 14th Dec	No S.A.A. drawn or issued. 2 Horses returned to No: 6 Mobile Section A.V.C. Harness Inspection. 9 p.m. Germans began to shell the town and at 9.45 p.m. withdrew all horses into safety at PONT de NIEPPE. 11.30 P.M. Shelling slackened and ceased; factory close by burning furiously. 12 (midnight) shelling recommenced vigorously; horses withdrawn to PONT de NIEPPE for the remainder of the night. No casualties. 1 Horse died of colic.	KBh
" 15th Dec	7 A.M. horses and men returned to The Billet. No S.A.A. issued or drawn. Received from Bazfield 2 Boxes of Cartridges Signal Light Blue Barth Ignition. Returned to be Div. Amm. Col. 28 Boxes (Loose S.A.A). 110 boxes of Empties. 5 Sacks. O.C. Train notified of dead horse for replacing.	KBh

(9 29 6) W 2794 100,000 8/14 H W V Forms/C. 2118/11.

WAR DIARY
or
INTELLIGENCE SUMMARY.
(Erase heading not required.)

Army Form C. 2118.

Hour, Date, Place	Summary of Events and Information	Remarks and references to Appendices
ARMENTIERES 16th & 17th Dec	No S.A.A. drawn. 5000 rounds SAA issued to Argyll Highlanders, 5000 rounds SAA 300 rounds Revolver to 5th Cameronians (Scottish Rifles) 2nd Lieut H.B. Yeoh returned from leave and took over Command of Ammunition Column from Lieut. R.O. Brooke-Murray. O.C.	Kolm.
17th Dec	No SAA drawn. 16 horses moved to 1st Middlesex. 1 horse of D secured as 14th not exchanged will 5th Scottish Rifles for a heavy draught.	wet
18 Dec	Issued 10 wire ropes SAA to R.W. Fusiliers. Horses inspected.	wet
19 Dec	Issued 16000 rounds to R.W. Fusiliers. 1 Heavy draught horse returned to V mobile Section. OC then informed by replacement.	wet
20th Dec	2 grooms rounds SAA drawn from MT section of A&SH. 8000 rounds issued to 1st Scottish Rifles and 16000 to 1st Middlesex Voluntary Church Parade held at R.W. Fusiliers.	wet
21 Dec	16000 rounds SAA issued to R.W. Fusiliers.	wet

Army Form C. 2118.

WAR DIARY
or
INTELLIGENCE SUMMARY.
(Erase heading not required.)

Instructions regarding War Diaries and Intelligence Summaries are contained in F.S. Regs., Part II. and the Staff Manual respectively. Title pages will be prepared in manuscript.

Hour, Date, Place	Summary of Events and Information	Remarks and references to Appendices
ARMENTIÈRES 22ᵈ Dec	4800 rounds issued to 1st Middlesex Harmer and Majors inspected. Weather opened.	wng
23ᵈ Dec	Issued 16,000 rounds to R.W. Fusiliers.	wng
24ᵗʰ Dec	Our visitors today from to Sir Sandhid hunter in the evening of men all biz, these also his servant all were in detail.	wng
25ᵗʰ Dec	No SAA drawn or issued. Royal Xmas card distributed also HRH Princess Mary's gifts. Church Parade held.	wng
26ᵗʰ Dec	57,000 rounds issued to C. Light Infantry, 18ᵗʰ Bde. Returned 56 boxes of rifles DOAC out drew 6000 rounds. 1 R.D. bone out to V. Milile. Section at 1 amount peened from Same gunner.	wng
" 19ᵗʰ Bde relieved by 18ᵗʰ by Odr 4 moves attached to Column. 1 HD hone all helow this alt		wng

(9 29 6) W 2794 100,000 8/14 HWV Forms/C. 2118/11.

Army Form C. 2118.

WAR DIARY
or
INTELLIGENCE SUMMARY.
(Erase heading not required.)

Instructions regarding War Diaries and Intelligence Summaries are contained in F. S. Regs., Part II. and the Staff Manual respectively. Title pages will be prepared in manuscript.

Hour, Date, Place	Summary of Events and Information	Remarks and references to Appendices
ARMENTIERES 27th Dec	no SAA drawn or moved. Voluntary Church Parade	wst
" 28th Dec	no SAA drawn or moved. Horses inspected and mules moved drawn with crowds to full use of lice.	
" 29th Dec	1 Box of Paraffin ammunition moved to A. & Sull. Highlanders. the horses clothing no SAA moved. Inspected by Lieut-Colonel ROBERTSON acting Brigadier General 19th Infy Bde.	wst
" 30th Dec		wst
" 31st Dec	no SAA drawn or moved.	wst

End of VOLUME V

CONFIDENTIAL.

121/4327

WAR DIARY

of

19th Infantry Brigade Ammunition Column

From 1st January 1915 – to 31st January 1915.

VOLUME VI.

Army Form C. 2118.

WAR DIARY
or
INTELLIGENCE SUMMARY.
(Erase heading not required.)

Instructions regarding War Diaries and Intelligence Summaries are contained in F.S. Regs., Part II. and the Staff Manual respectively. Title pages will be prepared in manuscript.

Hour, Date, Place	Summary of Events and Information	Remarks and references to Appendices
ARMENTIERES. 1st Jan.	50,000 rounds S.A.A. collected from Brigade units returned to railhead. Action in orders from Brigade 14th Jan 2lb. Proof proceeded to ammunition railhead ARGUES in search of hand grenades. Trench rations were drawn out were uncertain. Arrangements were made. Trench Ctee Civ A.C. to draw 250 grenades, 1 unit Cart Handles	W.S.F.
ARMENTIERES 2nd Jan	32,000 S.A.A. issued to 1st Middlesex, 250 grenades received. Ammunition Column received orders to move to new billet in RUE DES ACQUETS near the junction of road ERQUINHEM - ARMENTIERES Rd, the 19th Inf Bde relieving 16th Inf Bde in trenches. This move was completed in 3 days from waggons leaving to return to nearest S.A.A. & grenades.	W.S.F.
RUE DES ACQUETS 3rd Jan	32,000 rds SAA issued to 1st Middlesex. Grenades were requisitioned on district in quantities reported by Bde	

(9 29 6) W 2794 100,000 8/14 H W V   Forms/C. 2118/11.

Army Form C. 2118.

WAR DIARY
or
INTELLIGENCE SUMMARY.
(Erase heading not required.)

Instructions regarding War Diaries and Intelligence Summaries are contained in F. S. Regs., Part II. and the Staff Manual respectively. Title pages will be prepared in manuscript.

Hour, Date, Place		Summary of Events and Information	Remarks and references to Appendices
RUE DES ACQUETS	4th Jan	Hd. Qrs.	
"	"	No S.A.A. ammunition drawn. 2 Heavy drawers received	WD⅌
"	5th Jan	No S.A.A. issued or drawn. Billet in used as drawer was passed up from a painter. Painter was commenced to be put down as house hire to candidates munch; several matters etc.	WD⅌
"	6th Jan	Issued 12 rds of 1 mg Pistol Cartridges to R.W. Fusiliers. House hire etc continued.	WD⅌
"	7th Jan	Issued 16000 rds S.A.A. to 9th Staffords 17th Feb. 2 Heavy draught Horses received. 10 AM a Grenade Squad came from 2nd R.W. Fusiliers. Squad watched in method of preparing and discharging grenades.	WD⅌
"	8th Jan	10 AM Grenade Squad instructed. 2 r.n. Rifle & Accoutrement inspection. 4 p.m. 80 Hand grenades next to R.W. Fusiliers	WD⅌
"	9th Jan	No S.A.A. movent. House hire & guns were finished to day	WD⅌

WAR DIARY
or
INTELLIGENCE SUMMARY.
(Erase heading not required.)

Army Form C. 2118.

Hour, Date, Place	Summary of Events and Information	Remarks and references to Appendices
RUE DES ACQUETS, 10 Jan	3000 rds SAA to A. & S.H., Highlanders, Hannover Inspection. Hannover at present showing no ill effects from exceptionally bad weather.	
11 Jan	Grenade Squad from 1st Camerons instructed in use of time grenade.	WF
12 Jan	8 sacks home SAA returned to 6th Div. AC. 2nd Grenade Squad of 1st Camerons instructed. Sample line of 25. French hand grenades received.	WF
13 Jan	40 hand grenades (Toulet) issued to 1st Camerons. Experimental with French hand grenade not found.	WF
14 Jan	Received 1 case Very Pistol Cartridges, Rifle magazines.	WF
15 Jan	Moved 41000 rds SAA. Grenade Squad from 2nd Arg. & Sutt. Highlanders instructed.	WF
16 Jan	2 Boxes of Rifle Ammunit. (surplus) moved to N.S. Staffords. 2nd Grenade Squad instructed (A. & S.H.).	WF
17 Jan	Another Squad from (A. & S.H.) instructed. 2nd Hannover	WF

WAR DIARY
or
INTELLIGENCE SUMMARY.
(Erase heading not required.)

Army Form C. 2118.

Hour, Date, Place	Summary of Events and Information	Remarks and references to Appendices
RUE DES ACQUETS. 18 Jan	Inspection. 40 hgenade issued to Arg. & Sult. Highlanders. 2 boxes of Parabellum A. issued to 5th Cameronians. Received 5 packs horse SAA to 6th Our AC. 1 Heavy draught horse died of pneumonia. Standard of Horse Reg[?]	WBJ
19th Jan	Issued 50 rds "Very" Pistol A. to Arg. & Sult. Highlanders. 30 rds Very Pistol A. next to 19th Rdn HQ gn. Returned 4 packs horse SAA to 6th Cur AC. Received 52 hgenades hand, Irish & 2 boxes Very Pistol A. 1st hgenades Squad from 1st Middlesex instructed.	WBJ WBJ
20th Jan 21st Jan	Issued 100 rds SAA to Arg. & Sult. H. 20 rds of Very Pistol A. to 19th Rdn HQ gn. 2nd hgrenade Squad instructed from 1st Middlesex 2 from Rifle[?]	WBJ
22nd Jan 23rd Jan	No SAA issued or drawn. 40 rds Very Pistol A. next to 19th Rdn H. Gn. 20 rds to 5th Cameronians. 50 (Annual) Double Cylinder Hand Grenades received. 2 Boxes Very Pistol A received	WBJ WBJ

Army Form C. 2118.

WAR DIARY
or
INTELLIGENCE SUMMARY.
(Erase heading not required.)

Instructions regarding War Diaries and Intelligence Summaries are contained in F.S. Regs., Part II. and the Staff Manual respectively. Title pages will be prepared in manuscript.

Hour, Date, Place	Summary of Events and Information	Remarks and references to Appendices
RUE DES ACQUETS 24 Jan.	No S.A.A. issued or drawn. 9.15 PM Church Parade service held by C.F. 18th Field Amb. 2 P.M. Harness Inspection.	WD5
" 25 Jan.	No S.A.A. issued or drawn, New double cylinders & lot repairs reported not satisfactory.	WD5
" 26 Jan.	Issued 24,000 rds S.A.A. to 1st Connaughts, and 5 double cylinders had repairs to 1st Gordon Field Coy. R.E. re engineered purposes.	WD5
" 27 Jan.	Issued 16,000 rds S.A.A. to 1st Connaughts 2000 rds S.A.A. to A.S.+S.H. Returned to Ord. lorre S.A.R. & 6" Pist. A.C. Received 200 grenades Hand Smith lever Mark I. Issued 150 of same to 1st Middlesex. 100 to R.W.F. (85 in hand).	WD5
" 28 Jan.	Issued 32,000 to A.S.+S.H. & 1st Rifle Inspection.	WD5
" 29 Jan.	Received 150,000 rds S.A.A. ball & 6" Pist. AC.	WD5
" 30 Jan.	20 rd Very Pistol A. to A.S.+S.H. issued remaining hand grenades Smith (35) + 10 French	WD5

Army Form C. 2118.

WAR DIARY
or
INTELLIGENCE SUMMARY.
(Erase heading not required.)

Instructions regarding War Diaries and Intelligence Summaries are contained in F.S. Regs., Part II. and the Staff Manual respectively. Title pages will be prepared in manuscript.

Hour, Date, Place	Summary of Events and Information	Remarks and references to Appendices
QUE DES ACQUETS 30th Jan	hgrenades to 6.5 Cameronians.	wm3
" 31st Jan	no S.A.A. issued to drums. Known inspection 2 pm.	wm3
	END of VOLUME VI.	

CONFIDENTIAL.

121/4508

WAR DIARY

OF

19th Infantry Bde. Ammunition Column

From 1st February 1915 to 28th February 1915

VOLUME VII

Army Form C. 2118.

WAR DIARY
or
INTELLIGENCE SUMMARY.
(Erase heading not required.)

Instructions regarding War Diaries and Intelligence Summaries are contained in F.S. Regs., Part II. and the Staff Manual respectively. Title pages will be prepared in manuscript.

Hour, Date, Place	Summary of Events and Information	Remarks and references to Appendices
RUE DES ACQUETS 1st Feb	Issued 4000 rds SAA to 1st Seaforth Rifles. 16,000 to Argyll & Sutherland Highlanders. Received 400 double cylinder hand grenades	
2nd Feb	Issued SAA 1st S. Rifles 300 rounds Revolver A. to 2nd R.W.F.	WS.G
3rd Feb	Issued 20 rounds of Very Pistol Amm to Bde M. Gun	WS.G
4th Feb	Issued 16,000 rounds SAA to 1st Middlesex. 1000 rounds SAA to 2nd A.&S.H. 10000 to 5th S. Rifles. Received 29,000 rounds SAA from 2nd A.&S.H. all in good condition. Returned to 6th Divl A.C. 4 boxes blank + some rusted SAA. Rifle inspection held.	WS.G
5th Feb	Issued 48,000 rds SAA to 2nd R.W. Fusiliers. 16,000 to 1st Middlesex. 32,000 to 2nd R.W.F. 1000 rds to 2nd A.&S.H. 64 rds Very Pistol Amm - to Bde M. Gun.	WS.E
6th Feb	Issued 50 double cylinder grenades to each of following :- 1st & 6th S. Rifles & 2nd A.&S.H. N.C.Os of 2nd A.&S.H. + 1st S. Rifles instructed in use	

Forms/C. 2118/11.

Army Form C. 2118.

WAR DIARY
or
INTELLIGENCE SUMMARY.
(Erase heading not required.)

Instructions regarding War Diaries and Intelligence Summaries are contained in F.S. Regs., Part II. and the Staff Manual respectively. Title pages will be prepared in manuscript.

Hour, Date, Place	Summary of Events and Information	Remarks and references to Appendices
RUE DES ACQUETS		
7th Feb.	& preparation of Rumble English Hand Grenades. Issued 3000 rds SAA to 5th S. Rifles. 12 mich. bos hanson ingestion.	WRF
8th Feb.	Issued 2000 rds SAA to 3rd S. Rifles	WRF
9th	Issued 6000 to R.W.F., 2000 rds to A. & S.H. One G.V.M.S. heavy draught mare in foal returned to struck off Animal Register by order of V.O. 1/C Bde.	WRF
10 Feb.	2000 rds S.A.T. issued to 1st Scottish Rifles	WRF
11 Feb.	No S.A.T. issued or drawn. Rifle inspection.	WRF
12 Feb.	Received from 6th Div A.C. (MT. Section) 100000 rds SAA 30 Jamite Hand grenades. Returned to railhead 26 boxes & 2 sacks empties & horse rugs etc. Entrainment was returned by a de of Bde Hd Qrs 40000 rds SAA to all out to was con for grenades the	WRF
13 Feb.	Issued 120 double English grenades to 1st Middlesex & 60 to 5th S. Rifles.	WRF

Army Form C. 2118.

WAR DIARY
or
INTELLIGENCE SUMMARY.
(Erase heading not required.)

Instructions regarding War Diaries and Intelligence Summaries are contained in F.S. Regs., Part II. and the Staff Manual respectively. Title pages will be prepared in manuscript.

Hour, Date, Place	Summary of Events and Information	Remarks and references to Appendices
QUE DESA REGUETS 15 Feb.	Issued 16000 S.A.A. to 1st Middlesex. 100 Rouleau cylinder Hand grenades to R.W. Fusiliers. Various inspections.	unit
15 Feb.	60 rds Very Pistol Ammn to 5th S. Rifles + 48 rds to Bde. Md. Gun.	W.D.g
16 Feb.	No S.A.A. issue or drawn.	W.D.g
17 Feb.	50 detonators received from 6th Div. A.C. to replace the unreliable ones by Bde ?	W.D.g
18 Feb.	96 rds Very Pistol Ammn issued to 2nd A. & S.H. 240 rds V. Pistol A. drawn from 6th Div. A.C. Rifle + various other inspections.	W.D.g
19 Feb.	Issued 4000 rds S.A.A. to 2nd A. & S.H. 20 Rifle grenades (IA) to 1st S. Rifles	W.D.g
20 Feb.	Issued 20000 rds S.A.A. to 5th S. Rifles. 48 rds V. Pistol Ammn to 10 rifle grenades to 1st Scottish Rifles. 120 Smith Hand grenades drawn & 24 Jam Lift	

WAR DIARY
or
INTELLIGENCE SUMMARY.
(Erase heading not required.)

Army Form C. 2118.

Hour, Date, Place	Summary of Events and Information	Remarks and references to Appendices
QUE DES ACQUETS		
21st Feb.	Hand grenade received by order of 15th Bir. 4000 rds issued to 1st R.W.F. 16000 rds S.A.A. & one box of Revolver Amm. to 1st S. Rifles. 30 Limits Hand grenade received from 6th Div Ae. The 24 Isaytel Grenades received yesterday were 5-day.	WRF
22nd Feb.	Revealed by order of 6th Div. Harness inspection. Issued 16000 rds to 5th 1st Cameronians & 16000 rds S.A.A. to R.W. Fusiliers. 10 Hand grenade to B. 1st Middlesex Drew 150 000 rds S.A.A from 6th Div Ae. (MT Section) Returned to railhead 26 boxes 6 saddles empties & loose unfit S.A.A.	WRF
23rd Feb.	No S.A.A. issued or drawn. General Officer Commnts 19th Inf Bde inspected Ammunition Column 2.30pm.	WRF
24th Feb.	No S.A.A. issued or drawn.	WRF
25th Feb.	No S.A.A. issued or drawn. Rifle inspection.	WRF
26th Feb.	Issued 4000 rds S.A.A. to 1st S. Rifles & 7000 rds S.A.A.	WRF

Army Form C. 2118.

WAR DIARY
or
INTELLIGENCE SUMMARY.
(Erase heading not required.)

Instructions regarding War Diaries and Intelligence Summaries are contained in F.S. Regs., Part II. and the Staff Manual respectively. Title pages will be prepared in manuscript.

Hour, Date, Place	Summary of Events and Information	Remarks and references to Appendices
RUE DES ACQUETS	+ 48 rds Revolver Amm — to 6th g. Rifles	WRJ
27th Feb.	80 Smile Hand grenades received from 6 Div.	
	mil S.A.A. issued.	
28th Feb.	3000 rds S.A.A. + 60 J. Pistol Amm — issued to 2nd A & S.H. 50 Smile grenades to 5th S. Rifles 18 to 2nd A & S.H. Received 240 rds of Very Pistol Amm — + 6 boxes of Revolver Amm — from 6 Div. A.C. Harmer Range stick.	WRJ
	END OF VOLUME VII	WRJ

19th Bde Ammn Col
Vol VIII 1 — 31.3.15

CONFIDENTIAL

WAR DIARY

of

19th Infantry Brigade Ammunition Column.

From March 1st 1915 to March 31st 1915

VOLUME VIII

Army Form C. 2118.

WAR DIARY
or
INTELLIGENCE SUMMARY.
(Erase heading not required.)

Instructions regarding War Diaries and Intelligence Summaries are contained in F. S. Regs., Part II. and the Staff Manual respectively. Title pages will be prepared in manuscript.

Hour, Date, Place	Summary of Events and Information	Remarks and references to Appendices
(ERQUINGEM)		
RUE DES ACQUETS March 1st	Drew 114 Jenks grenades from 6th Div A.C. Issued 16000 rds SAA to 5th S. Rifles.	
" March 2nd	Drew 120 Double Cylinder grenades.	wng
" March 3rd	Drew 122 D. Cylinder grenades & 70 Jenks Hand grenades.	wng
" March 4th	Drew 42 Jenks Hand grenades from 6th Div A.C. Issued 2000 rds SAA and 300 rds Revolver Amm. to 2nd R.W. Fusiliers.	wng
" March 5th	Welshing Rifles inspection	wng
" March 5th	Issued 20 Jenks grenades to 1st S. Rifles	wng
" March 6th	Issued 4000 rds SAA to 2nd R.W. Fusiliers & 12 Rifle grenades	wng
" March 7th	Issued 12 rds Very Pistol cartridges & 20 Double Cylinder grenades with fuze to 2nd R.W. Fusiliers. Barwen inspection	wng
" March 8th	Drew 100 Rifle grenades. Issued 20 ditto to 2nd R.W.F.	wng
" March 9th	Issued 2000 rds SAA & 120 safety lighters for D. Cylinder grenades to 1st Scottish Rifles.	wng
" March 10	Issued 42,000 rds SAA to 2nd A&SH	wng
" March 11	Issued 2000 rds SAA & 12 safety lighters to 2nd A & S. Highrs	wng

Army Form C. 2118.

WAR DIARY
or
INTELLIGENCE SUMMARY.
(Erase heading not required.)

Instructions regarding War Diaries and Intelligence Summaries are contained in F. S. Regs., Part II. and the Staff Manual respectively. Title pages will be prepared in manuscript.

Hour, Date, Place	Summary of Events and Information	Remarks and references to Appendices
RUE DES REQUETS		
March 12th	Rifle inspection.	
	Served guns rds SAA, 8 O. infantry & 8 trench hand grenades to 2nd R.W.F., 3200 rds SAA & 46 rds of Very Pistol Cartridge to 1st S. Rifles. 5000 rds & 2 A+H. SAA	w.g.
March 13th	To 1st Middlesex 200 rds Perrelere Ammn, 750 rds V. Pistol Cartridge. To 1st S. Rifles — 16000 rds SAA, 100 rds V Pistol. To 2nd R.W. Fusiliers 264 Trench grenades. To 2nd A+S.H. 21000 rds SAA. To 5th S. Rifles 60 rds V. Pistol Cartridges.	w.g.
March 14th	Issued to 1st Middlesex 50 Smith & 10 double cylinder grenades. To 2nd A+S.H. 24 rds of V. Pistol Ammn. Hansen mag,	w.g.
March 15th	Over 50000 rds SAA from 6th Div. A.S. Issued 50 Rifle grenades to 1st Middlesex & 1 Box of Perrelere Ammn. 19th Bde H/d Gun Received 6 Light Draught Horses in lieu of 3 heavy Draught deficient from 6th Div. Train. Entered in H. Regis.	w.g.

WAR DIARY
or
INTELLIGENCE SUMMARY.
(Erase heading not required.)

Army Form C. 2118.

Instructions regarding War Diaries and Intelligence Summaries are contained in F. S. Regs., Part II. and the Staff Manual respectively. Title pages will be prepared in manuscript.

Hour, Date, Place	Summary of Events and Information	Remarks and references to Appendices
RUE DES ACQUETS March 16	Issued 12 Rifle Grenades to 1st S. Rifles, 12 Bundles Sandbags etc to 1st Middlesex, 10 O.C. It Grenades + 25 Joints to It Grenades to 2nd R.W. Fusiliers. 16000 rds S.A.A., 1st S. Rifles	
March 17	Issued 300 rds Revolver Ammn — F.M. Pole Hd Qs, + 7000 rds S.A.A. to 1st Gordon Field Cny R.E.	W.S.G.
March 18	Issued 1000 rds S.A.A., D2 + B. + S.H., 700 rds Revolver Ammn to 1st S. Rifles. Weekly rifle inspection	W.S.G.
March 19	Nil S.A.A. etc. issued or drawn	W.S.G.
March 20	Recd 100 rifle grenades + 1056 rds (6 boxes) Revolver Ammn from 6th Div. A.C. Issued 16000 rds S.A.A. + 3 Boxes of Revolver A. to 1st Middlesex. 1 Box Revolver A. to 2nd A.Y.S.H.	W.S.G.
March 21	Issued 5000 rds S.A.A. to 1st Gordons & 1st Cny R.E. 12 mm Rifle S.A.A. war grenades + accoutrements recd at 2nd Army Order. Recd 120 rds V. Pistol Cartridges from 6th Div AC Weekly Hammer inspection	W.S.G.
March 22	Issued 1000 rds S.A.A. to 2nd A. + S.H.	W.S.G.

Army Form C. 2118.

WAR DIARY
or
INTELLIGENCE SUMMARY.
(Erase heading not required.)

Instructions regarding War Diaries and Intelligence Summaries are contained in F. S. Regs., Part II. and the Staff Manual respectively. Title pages will be prepared in manuscript.

Hour, Date, Place	Summary of Events and Information	Remarks and references to Appendices
QUE GES ASQUETS March 23rd	Issued 34,000 rds S.A.A, 36 H. grenade Trench mort 6 sect detonators to 1st S. Rifles. 16000 rds S.A.A to 1st Middlesex. 2000 rds S.A.A to 2nd A. & S.H.	
March 24th	Drew 100000 rds S.A.A & 100 Smoke Hand grenades from 6th Res. AC. Issued 2000 rds S.A.A to 2nd A.T.S.H.	W.S.F.
March 25th	Issued 12 D. Cylinder grenades & 13 H. grenade Tombs to 5th S. Rifles. Exchanged 1 pair of Heavy Draught mlt O.C. Train 19th Bde. Watched rifle inspection	W.S.F.
March 26th	Issued 51 Rifle grenades to 2nd R.W. Fusiliers	W.S.F. W.S.F.
March 27th	Issued 10000 rds S.A.A to 5th S. Rifles & O.C. & Train grenades to the 1st Middlesex	W.S.F.
March 28th	Issued 1 lme Pendun ie. to 2nd A.T.S.H. Exchanged 1 H. Draught horse & 1 pair of E.D for 1 pair of H. Draught from O.C. Train 19th Bde. Weekly Harness inspection	
March 29th	Issued 32000 rds S.A.A to 2nd R.W.F. 1000 rds S.A.A & 12	W.S.F.

Army Form C. 2118.

WAR DIARY
or
INTELLIGENCE SUMMARY.
(Erase heading not required.)

Instructions regarding War Diaries and Intelligence Summaries are contained in F.S. Regs., Part II. and the Staff Manual respectively. Title pages will be prepared in manuscript.

Hour, Date, Place	Summary of Events and Information	Remarks and references to Appendices
	Double explosive to generate K 2nd A & B.H. 8 double cylinder & Tonite bombs. 16 detonators & safety fuses for O.C. grenades to each of 1st & 5th S. Rifles. Instructions in accordance with instructions from Fld Gen Hqrs 20,000 rds S.A.A. to 5th S. Rifles	W.S.
Aue Des. August 3. March 3?	Issued 2000 rds S.A.A. & 3 double cyld grenade to 2nd Bn S.L.H. 36-day received orders to count all S.A.A. of K & 14 M & V.II. Ale rep/s ordered to return same as it was thought to be defective	W.S.
March 31st	Issued 2000 rds S.A.A. & 1st S. Rifle 13,000 rds S.A.A. to 1st Middlesex. Total 15,14 Mks VII received & found in stock 73,000 rds.	W.S.

END OF VOLUME VIII

CONFIDENTIAL.

WAR DIARY

of

19th Infantry Brigade Ammunition Column

From 1st April 1915 to 30th April 1915

VOLUME IX

Army Form C. 2118.

WAR DIARY
or
INTELLIGENCE SUMMARY.
(Erase heading not required.)

Instructions regarding War Diaries and Intelligence Summaries are contained in F.S. Regs., Part II. and the Staff Manual respectively. Title pages will be prepared in manuscript.

Hour, Date, Place	Summary of Events and Information	Remarks and references to Appendices
(ERGUINGEM) 10.15 RUE DES ACQUETS 1st April	250 Mills grenades. Issued 4000 rds S.A.A. & 100 double cylinder grenades to 1st Cameroonians. 8000 rds S.A.A. & 2nd Ars. & S.H. 10 D. Cylinder + grenades to 1st Middlesex. & H grenades Twin & O.C.H. grenades to 2nd R.W.F milliers.	w/g
2nd April	Drew 9000 rds S.A.A., 150 double cylinder h. grenades. 600 rds Return Ammn. from 1st Divs inc. 4000 rds S.A.A. returned by 2nd Ars. & S.H.	w/g
3rd April	8000 rds S.A.A. issued to 2nd Ars. S.H. 10 Twin grenades to 1st Cameroonians	w/g
4th April	5000 rds S.A.A. issued to 5th Cameroonians. Widely Harman Inspection	w/g
5th April	3000 rds S.A.A & 24 rds Very Pistol Cartridges issued to 2nd Ars & S.H. 50 rds V. Pistol Cartridges + 24 rifle grenades to 2nd R.W. Fusiliers.	w/g
6th April	Drew 50 rifle grenades for 6" cur. A.C. + issued to 5 i/R Withdrew	w/g
7th April	Issued 60 boxes S.A. which were taken up by major & dumped — the machine gun emplacements by the 2nd Durham Milliers.	w/g

WAR DIARY
or
INTELLIGENCE SUMMARY.
(Erase heading not required.)

Army Form C. 2118.

Hour, Date, Place	Summary of Events and Information	Remarks and references to Appendices
RUE DES ACQUETS, 8th April	By Brigade orders, 2 bomber equipt on reached 15. 1st Middlesex Rifle grenades. 8 Trench M. O.C. grenades issued to 1st Cameronians. 20 O.C. grenades to 1st Middx. 1000 rds S.A.A. Fort Arty & S.H. now issued to latter in charge at 73 brewery, 14/14 S.A.A. Withdrawn from battalions last month.	msg
9th April	S.A.A. issued — 20,000 rds to 1st Cameronians, 16,000 rds to 2nd R.W. Fusiliers, 5000 rds to 7 Trench grenades to S. S. Cameronians, 4000 rds to 1st Middlesex. 3000 rds + 60 V. Pistol cartridges to 2nd Argyll S.H.	msg
10th April	Over 120,000 rds S.A.A., 150 Trench grenades + 120 rd V. Pistol cartridge from 6th D.W.A.C. issued 19,000 rds S.A.A. to each of 2nd R.W.F. 1st Cameronian, 200 Safety lights to 2nd A + S.H	msg
11th April	Issued 2000 rds S.A.A. to 1st Middlesex. Wiring Hessian supplied to	msg
12th April	22,000 rds S.A.A. + 7 Rifle grenades issued to 1st Cameronians	msg

WAR DIARY or INTELLIGENCE SUMMARY

Army Form C. 2118.

Hour, Date, Place	Summary of Events and Information	Remarks and references to Appendices
RUE DES ACQUETS 12th April (cont'd)	4000 rds SAA to 2nd R.W. Fusiliers, 7 Tools & P.C. grenades to 1st Middx	
13th April	52,000 rds SAA to 1st Cameronians	WD ✓
14th April	Issued 10,000 rds SAA to 2nd A&SH. 36 D.C. & 9 Tools, 70 Safety fighters, 40 Very Pistol Cartridges to 1st Cameronians. Wearing Rifle inspection.	WD ✓
15th April	Drew 100,000 rds SAA + 100 D.C. H grenades from 6 Div AC. Issued 4000 rds SAA to 5th Cameronians	WD ✓
16th April	13,000 rds SAA to 2nd A&S S.H.	WD ✓
17th April	No S.A.A. issued or drawn. 4 Drivers M.S. joined unit	WD ✓
18th April	16,000 rds SAA to 1st Middlesex. Weekly Iron Inspection	WD ✓
19th April	2000 rds S.A.A. Issued to 1st Cameronians, 9000 rds to 1st Middlesex, 6 rifle grenades & 24 Rds Very Cart to 2nd R.W. Fusiliers	
20th April	Issued 18,000 rds to 2nd R.W. Fusiliers, 8 O.E. & T mile grenades, 16 Safety fighters to 1st Middlesex, 10 T mile &	WD ✓

WAR DIARY
or
INTELLIGENCE SUMMARY.
(Erase heading not required.)

Army Form C. 2118.

Hour, Date, Place	Summary of Events and Information	Remarks and references to Appendices
QUE DES ACQUETS		
21st April	10 O.C. Grenades to 2nd Argylls S.H.	wef
22nd April	100 rds V Pistol to 5th Cameronians. Weekly rifle Inspection	wef
	2000 rds SAA issued to 2nd Arg & S.H. 5 Tents & 5 O.E. Grenades	
	to 2nd R.W. Fusiliers. 5 rifle grenades to 5th Cameronians	
23rd April	10 O.C. H. Grenades to 1st Middlesex. 1 H.D. issued returned	wef
	to V. Malcolm Jutrio	
24th April	23,000 rds SAA, 5 Tents + 5 O.E. Grenades 450 rafts rifles,	
	4 rifle grenades issued to 5th Cameronians. 32 rds in	
	SAA to 1st Middlesex, 52 rds to 5th Cameronians,	
	16,000 rds SAA to 2nd Arg & S.H. 14 Tents + 8 D.C. H grenades	
	to 2nd Q.W. Fusiliers.	
25th April	1000 rds SAA issued to 2nd Arg S.H. to practice trench mortar	wef
26th April	Received 500 foam got grenades made by R.E. from 1st Vth	wef
	Middlesex Regt. Issued 10,000 rds SAA 200 rds Revolver to	
	5th Cameronians. 5 Tents grenades & 32 Grenade Pennies	
	to 5th Middlesex. 4 Trench grenades & 32 grenade Pennies	

WAR DIARY
or
INTELLIGENCE SUMMARY.
(Erase heading not required.)

Army Form C. 2118.

Hour, Date, Place	Summary of Events and Information	Remarks and references to Appendices
	To 1st Camerons	
Que Des Aequets 27th April	50 Rifle grenades issued to H.Q. Coy 16th Middlx. 16000 rds S.A.A. 50 rds V. Pistol & rifle grenades to 2nd R.W. Fusiliers	WYF
28th April	30 Tools 30 P.E. grenades 21 Cartridges for Tools to 4/12 rds V. Pistol to R.W. Fusiliers. 16 R.E. Jam-pot grenades to 1st Middlesex + 12 to 5th Camerons. P. Completion	WYF
29th April	16000 rds S.A.A., 1 doz. Revolver Amm. + 30 rds V. Pistol to 2 Arg'll H. 16000 rds S.A.A. & 6 Rifle grds to R.W.F. 2000 rds S.A.A. to 1st Camerons. 8000 to 5th Camerons.	WYF
30th April	Issued 2000 rds S.A.A. 16 Tools Jam-pot grenades to 1st Camerons + 16 R.E. Jam-pot grenades to 5th Camerons.	WYF
	End of Volume IX	

121/5536

19th Brigade Ammⁿ Colⁿ

Vol X 1 — 31.5.15

CONFIDENTIAL.

WAR DIARY

OF

19th Infantry Brigade Ammunition Column.

From 1st May 1915 to 31st May 1915

VOLUME X

WAR DIARY
INTELLIGENCE SUMMARY
(Erase heading not required.)

Army Form C. 2118.

Instructions regarding War Diaries and Intelligence Summaries are contained in F.S. Regs., Part II. and the Staff Manual respectively. Title pages will be prepared in manuscript.

Hour, Date, Place	Summary of Events and Information	Remarks and references to Appendices
ERQUINGHEM RUE DES ACQUETS 1st May	Issued 48 Very Pistol cartridges to 1st Cameronians, 16 Jampot RE grenades & 4 Toulite grenades to 2nd R.W. Fusiliers, and 300 rounds Revolver Amm. to 2nd Argyll & Suth. Highlanders.	wsf
2nd May	Drew & issued Revolver Amm. & 2 Lucas Very Pistol cartridges from 6th Div A.C. Issued 16 Jampot R.E. grenades, 4 Toulite grenades, 30 English & 4 wine grenade hairbrush to 2nd R.W. Fusiliers. 1 Box of Revolver Amm. to 2nd R. & S.H. 8000 rounds SAA to 1st Cameronians. Weekly Ammun. Inspection.	
3rd May	Issued 4 Rifle grenades to 1st Cameronians. 1 Steam	wsf
4th May	Draught horse received from 6th Div Mob. Section 68000 rounds SAA issued as Brigade Reserve	wsf
5th May	Drew 16000 rounds SAA from 6th Div A.C. Issued 8000 rdrs to 1st S. Rifles, 18 grenades T units to 1st Middlesex Weekly Rifle & M.G. Inspection	wsf
6th May	Issued 4 rdrs Very Pistol to 2nd R.W. Fusiliers. 10000 rdrs SAA 51 Toulite, 36 Cudgels cycles & 20 Jampot grenades to 1st S. Rifles	wsf

WAR DIARY or INTELLIGENCE SUMMARY

Army Form C. 2118.

(Erase heading not required.)

Hour, Date, Place	Summary of Events and Information	Remarks and references to Appendices
RUE DES ACQUETS 7th May	Drew 100 Trench & 100 Cordite English grenades from 6th Div A.C. Issued 32000 rds S.A.A. 20 Trench & 1 C.E. grenades to 2nd R.W. Fusiliers. 20 Trench grenades to 1st Middlesex.	
" 8th May	Issued 20000 rds S.A.A. to 2nd R.W. Fusiliers, 20000 rds to 5th S. Rifles, 1000 rds to 2nd A.&S.H.	W.O.J.
" 9th May	Drew 200 grenades, Trench from 6th Div A.C. Issued 32000 rds S.A.A. to 2nd R.W. Fusiliers. 16000 rds to 4th A.&S.H. 7000 rds to 5th S. Rifles. 48 grenades Trench to 1st Middlesex Regt. 24 rounds Very Pistol to Bde. H.Q. Qm. Weekly Itemn. Imperturbable.	W.O.J.
" 10th May	Drew 8000 rds S.A.A. from 6th Div A.C. Issued 48 Trench grenades to 1st Cameronians & 24 to 5th S. Rifles, 1000 rds to A.&S.H.	W.O.J.
" 11th May	Issued 4000 rds S.A.A. to 2nd A.&S.H. 24 Trench grenades to 1st Cameronians.	W.O.J.
" 12th May	Issued 8000 rds S.A.A. & 4 Cordite English grenades to 1 Cameronians. 300 rds Revolver Amn. to 2nd A.&S.H.	W.O.J.

Army Form C. 2118.

WAR DIARY
or
INTELLIGENCE SUMMARY.
(Erase heading not required.)

Instructions regarding War Diaries and Intelligence Summaries are contained in F.S. Regs., Part II. and the Staff Manual respectively. Title pages will be prepared in manuscript.

Hour, Date, Place	Summary of Events and Information	Remarks and references to Appendices
RUE DES REQUETS 13 May	6 grenades Twist to 5th S. Rifles, Rifles + 1LC inspection	wsf
" 14th May	Nil inved or drawn	wsf
" " 15th May	2000 rds SAA issued to 2nd A.& S.H.	wsf
" " 15th May	Nil issued or drawn	wsf
" " 16th May	Issued 32000 rds SAA to 1st Middlesex, 10000 rds SAA to 5th S. Rifles. Watch drawn inspection	wsf
" " 17th May	Nil issued or drawn	wsf
" " 18th May	Drew 8000 rds SAA + 30 rifle grenades from 6th Div A.C.	wsf
" " 19th May	Issued 20 Rifle grenades to 2nd R.W. Fusiliers, 16 sandpit R.E. grenades to 1st Middlesex & 6 Twist grenades 15 S Cameronians. Webley Rifle + 1LC inspection	wsf
" " 20th May	Nil issued or drawn	wsf
" " 21st May	Issued 16000 rds S.A.A. + 48 rds Very Pistol Ammn to 1st Cameronians. 10000 rds SAA to 2nd A. & S.H., 32 sandpit 8 Rifle grenades	wsf
" " 22nd May	R.E. grenades to 2nd R.W. Fusiliers. 24 grenades Sandpit R.E. issued to 5th S. Rifles	wsf

Army Form C. 2118.

WAR DIARY
or
INTELLIGENCE SUMMARY.
(Erase heading not required.)

Instructions regarding War Diaries and Intelligence Summaries are contained in F.S. Regs., Part II. and the Staff Manual respectively. Title pages will be prepared in manuscript.

Hour, Date, Place	Summary of Events and Information	Remarks and references to Appendices
RUE DES ACQUETS.		
23rd May	Nil issued or drawn. Between inspection.	Eng
24th May	1000 rds S.A.A. issued to 5-S. Rifles. 2000 rds B 2nd A&S.H.	Eng
25th May	Nil issued or drawn.	Eng
26th May	64 lumps of R.E. Ingredients issued to 5, 1st S. Rifles + 16 to 2nd R.W. Fusiliers. Weekly Rifles & kit inspection.	Eng
27th May	Nil issued or drawn.	Eng
28th May	Issued 32000 rds S.A.A. B 2nd R.W. Fusiliers. 24 T mile + 6 Double cylinder grenades. B 2nd A. & S.H.	Eng
29th May	Issued 12000 rds S.A.A. B 2nd A. & S.H.	Eng
30th May	Issued 16000 rds S.A.A. B 2nd A. & S.H.	Eng
31st May	Nil issued or drawn. Weekly Between inspection.	Eng

END OF VOLUME X

27TH DIVISION
19TH INFY BDE

19TH BDE AMMN COLUMN
JUN - AUG 1915

27th Division.

WAR DIARY

19th INFANTRY BRIGADE AMMUNITION COLUMN.

J U N E

1 9 1 5

CONFIDENTIAL.

19th Brigade

WAR DIARY

OF

19th Infantry Brigade Ammunition Column

From 1st June 1915 to 30th June 1915

VOLUME XI

Army Form C. 2118.

WAR DIARY
or
INTELLIGENCE SUMMARY
(Erase heading not required.)

Instructions regarding War Diaries and Intelligence Summaries are contained in F. S. Regs., Part II. and the Staff Manual respectively. Title pages will be prepared in manuscript.

Hour, Date, Place	Summary of Events and Information	Remarks and references to Appendices
ERQUINGHEM 1st June	Issued 24 RE grenades to 1st Leicesters. Issued over 114 Lt Grenades No 2 (Tennis) from 1st Middlesex.	W.E.
2nd June	Received from 27th Div A.C. 12000 rds S.A.A. Manual. 150 Lt grenades No 2 to 1st Middlesex.	W.E.
3rd June	Issued 16000 rds SAA to 2nd A. & S.H., 3000 to 5th S. Rifles. 3 t No 2 & 9 No 9 (Pauls cylindricals) grenades to 2nd R.W.F	W.E.
4th June	Nil in and or drawn.	W.E.
5th June	52000 rds SAA to RW Fusiliers, 60 rds Very Pistol to 2nd A & S.H. 30 RE grenades to 5th S. Rifles	W.E.
6th June	Nil issued or drawn.	W.E.
7th June	16000 rds SAA to 2nd R.W.F, 4000 rds SAA to 2nd Argyll S.H.	W.E.
8th June	28000 rds SAA to 5th S. Rifles. Received 80 No 2 grenades from R.E. Parle.	W.E.
9th June	24 RE grenades & 9000 rds SAA to 5th S. Rifles. Withdrew from 2nd Army 6 G.S Pinhard Wagons and	W.E.

Forms/C. 2118/11.

Army Form C. 2118.

WAR DIARY
or
INTELLIGENCE SUMMARY.
(Erase heading not required.)

Instructions regarding War Diaries and Intelligence Summaries are contained in F.S. Regs., Part II. and the Staff Manual respectively. Title pages will be prepared in manuscript.

Hour, Date, Place	Summary of Events and Information	Remarks and references to Appendices
	Bombs were received and added to established matches 21 which in all. To inspected Prov. War Establishment was submitted for consideration.	
RUE DES ACQUETS 10th June	24 R.E. Grenades & 5" S Rifles. 1 Box Carbine Amm. 1st Middx.	W.T.F
" 11th June	8000 rds SAA to 1st Cameronians 20 Rifle Grenades to 1st R.Hs. + S. Lt. Gren. 20000 rds SAA to 21st R.I.	W.T.F
" 12th June	Over from R.E. Pontoon - 50 No 12 (Bom) grenades 6 no 6 & no 1. (Service Pattern) Smooth & Rub't & fused Very light to R.Sn. 1st Qn.	W.T.F
" 13th June	Moved 35 V. Pistols to 1st Middlesex, 40 R.E. Grenade & 5" S. Rifles	W.T.F
" 14th June	48 R.E. Grenades & 5"S g Rifles & 24 to 1st Middlesex.	W.T.F
" 15th June	24 R.E. Grenades to 1st Middlesex, 14000 rds SAA to R.W.F.	W.T.F
	12000 rds SAA to R.+S.H. 2000 rds 1st Cameronians	
" 16th June	14000 rds SAA to 1st R.W.F	W.T.F
" 17th June	12000 rds SAA to 2 R.+H.S. 24 Rds V Pistol + 20 Rifle	W.T.F

WAR DIARY
or
INTELLIGENCE SUMMARY.
(Erase heading not required.)

Army Form C. 2118.

Instructions regarding War Diaries and Intelligence Summaries are contained in F.S. Regs., Part II. and the Staff Manual respectively. Title pages will be prepared in manuscript.

Hour, Date, Place	Summary of Events and Information	Remarks and references to Appendices
RDE DES ACQUETS 18th June	Grenades 15 & 2 A & S.H.	WJT
" 19th June	23 Rifle grenades to RWF. 600 rds SAA to 5th S. Rifles. Received 20 grens rds SAA from 27th Div R.E.	WJT
" 19th " pm	Grens 40. No 1, 40 No 2 Grenades & 120 rds Very Pistol, 24 Very Pistol from A&SH. 1 Right draught Horse despatched to V.M. Section.	WJT
" 20th June	Grens 50 & 2.7 and muzzle covers issued. 20 rds & 2x & 16000 rds SAA to RWF. 10000 rds SAA to 5th S. Rifles.	WJT
" 21st "	1200000 gr SAA out 36 Very light. 5 2nd A & S.H.	WJT
" 22nd June	Grens 15 Rifle Grenades from R.E. Park.	WJT
" 23rd "	Grens 20 Rifle Grenades Issued. 12 R.E. Grenades & 13 Mid + 5 No 2 & A & S.H. 44 rds Very Pistol to 1st Cameron.	WJT
" 24th June	Issued 16000 rds SAA & 1st Cameron. 5000 rds to A&SH.	WJT
" "	2000 rds to 5 5th S. Rifles	WJT
" 25th June	Grens 20 Rifle Grenades	WJT

Army Form C. 2118.

WAR DIARY
or
INTELLIGENCE SUMMARY.
(Erase heading not required.)

Hour, Date, Place	Summary of Events and Information	Remarks and references to Appendices
Aue des Acquets 26/June	1000 rds S.A.A. to 1st S. Rifles	wng
" 27/June	Nil issued or drawn.	
" 28 June	20000 rds S.A.A. to 5" S. Rifles, 9600 2 Grenades to 2nd A.S.A.S.M.	wng
" 29 June	10000 rds SAA to 5" S Rifles.	wng
" 30 June	25 Rifle grenades to 2nd R.W. Fusiliers	wng
	END OF VOLUME XI	

27th Division.

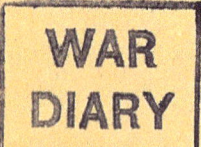

19th INFANTRY BRIGADE AMMUNITION COLUMN.

J U L Y

1 9 1 5

121/6308

"19th Division"

"CONFIDENTIAL"

WAR DIARY

OF

AMMUNITION COLUMN 19th INFANTRY BRIGADE

FROM 1-7-15 TO 31-7-15

VOLUME XII

WAR DIARY
or
INTELLIGENCE SUMMARY.
(Erase heading not required.)

Army Form C. 2118.

Hour, Date, Place	Summary of Events and Information	Remarks and references to Appendices
ERQUINGHEM.		
RUE DES ACQUETS 1st July 1915	Issued 10 Rifle grenades to 5th S. Rifles.	WST
" " 2nd July	Issued 16000 rds S.A.A. to 2nd R.W.F.	WST
" " 3rd July	Issued 16000 S.A.A. to 2nd R.W.F. and 276 rds Revolver	WST
" " 4th July	Ammn. 21,000 rds to 1st Cameronians 32000 rds S.A.A. to 1st Arg. & S. H. 1000 rds to 1st Middlesex	WST
" " 5th July	10 No. Hand grenades 25 Rifle grenades to 5th S. Rifles. 1 Light Gun sight received from 27th Div. Train	WST
" " 6th July	Issued 8000 rds SAA to 5th S.Rifles 5000 rds to 1st Cameronians 5000 rds to 2nd Arg & S.H. 5000 to R.W.F. 4000 1st Middlesex. 11 boxes to Bde Reserve + 24 rds Very lights to Bde. 116 Gr. Guns 12000 rds SAA for 27th Div. Res.	
" " 7th July	1 Heavy Oranuff lamp returned to Vet. M. Section	WST
" " 8th July	16000 rds SAA + 5 Rifle grenades to 1st Middlesex, 16000 rds + bombs to 5th S Rifles 5th S Rifles	WST

(9 29 6) W 2794 100,000 8/14 H W V   Forms/C. 2118/11.

Army Form C. 2118.

WAR DIARY
or
INTELLIGENCE SUMMARY.
(Erase heading not required.)

Instructions regarding War Diaries and Intelligence Summaries are contained in F.S. Regs., Part II. and the Staff Manual respectively. Title pages will be prepared in manuscript.

Hour, Date, Place	Summary of Events and Information	Remarks and references to Appendices
RUE DES ACQUETS 9th July	not drawn in west	w.s.d.
10th July	not drawn in west	w.s.d.
11th July	40 no 1 & 5 no 12 F & S. Rifle 20 no 12 R.W.F.	w.s.d.
12th July	11 cwrds S.A.A., N.C.R. n.b. Very lights 6 No 12 grenades 15 2 Boxes S.H. Bombs S.A.A. 5 " Cameronians	w.s.d.
13th July	3000 n.b S.A.A. F. 2nd R.W.F.	w.s.d.
14th July	54 n.s. Very Cart.d Ammo to R.W. Fusiliers	w.s.d.
15th July	Issued 40 Rifle grenades 120 n.b Very lights from 27th Div R.E.	w.s.d.
16th July	Not moved or shown	w.s.d.
17th July	Received notification that 4th Brigade would be relieved at 30th July by 14th near STEENWERCK	w.s.d.
18th July	wef 19th - 20th	
	Orders received that Ammn Column were not to move Motor Rolls, but await present billets	w.s.d.
19th July	Over the following grenade Stores from 27th R.E.	

Forms/C. 2118/11.

WAR DIARY or INTELLIGENCE SUMMARY

Army Form C. 2118.

(Erase heading not required.)

Hour, Date, Place	Summary of Events and Information	Remarks and references to Appendices
RUE DES REQUETS 20/July	Posta, 144 hr 3, Q 6 M 5, 80 Mob, 100 hrs 9, 100 Rifle Grenades 800 Jugo Rifles, 24 Fathom Amn + 600 rds Very Lights. Projects relieved Nil moved or known	WSt
21st July	Received notification that Punjab would relieve 154" Bde near LAVENTIE on night of 23rd-24th	WSt
22nd July	Orders received to proceed on morning of 24th to near ALLEZ ST LE NOUVEAU MONDE. Lt. Col. Drancole home died of Colic + was blanched at 8. Km. Column marched at 9.30 PM Via ERQUINGHEM - BAC-ST-MAUR - BAILEY to LE NOUVEAU MONDE	WSt
23rd July		WSt
LE NOUVEAU MONDE 24 July	Moved 32 wds SAA to 2d My + S.H.	WSt
25th July	Moved 32000 rds SAA + 90 rds V. lights to 2d Aug & S.H.	WSt
26th July	100,000 rds to S.H. drawn, but was great difficulty eventually obtained from 8th Dis. A.C. would not supply.	WSt

8th Div. A.C. would not supply. Eventually obtained from

Army Form C. 2118.

WAR DIARY
or
INTELLIGENCE SUMMARY.
(Erase heading not required.)

Instructions regarding War Diaries and Intelligence Summaries are contained in F. S. Regs., Part II. and the Staff Manual respectively. Title pages will be prepared in manuscript.

Hour, Date, Place	Summary of Events and Information	Remarks and references to Appendices
	9 Bdr. R.C. R.F.A. Report was made Steward.	
	Bdr. led Q^{rs} & eventuals outlying this were given	
	km 8th Div. A.C. 15 ampts 18" Hr Hdr R.C.	
	20 Red Rockets drawn from 8th Div Bomber Depot & issued	
	20 K 2nd Argyll H., 10 to 2nd R.W.T. 6 to 2 & 6 to 5	W.T
	Kth & Ay & K.H.	
LE NOUVEAU MONDE 27/July	Red. Q2 No 3 grenades for 1st Div Scout Report. Much	
	6 of each type of grenade & 6 rifle grenades to Bdr led	
	Q^{rs}	W.T
" 28/July	Captain W. B. F.ROOTS went on about leave 15 days and	
	handed over command of Army Col. man to Lieut M.	
	PAKENHAM at 12 noon. Received 280 Bethune & 75 Mog	
28th July	Bombs from 1st Middlesex	N.A.P
29th July	Rec. from 8 upin O.C 26 No1, 40 No6, & 46 Pitchr No 3 grenades. Rec from	
	Argyll & Sutherland Highlanders 200 Bethune grenades. Rec & issued	
	Column 32 Red Rockets, Issued 33 Red Rockets to Middlesex Regt &	
	16 to 5th Medirl Rifles."	N.M.P

Army Form C. 2118.

WAR DIARY
or
INTELLIGENCE SUMMARY.
(Erase heading not required.)

Hour, Date, Place	Summary of Events and Information	Remarks and references to Appendices
Nouveau Monde		
30th July	Rec'd 8th Div A.C. 40 No 2, 46 No 3 Rifles Grenades. 70 R.O.S Trench Mortar 1.5" 30 grenades.	
	Issued 30 R.O.S Very Pistol to 5th K.S. Rifles to 1st Middlesex	M.M.P
31st July	Rec from 5th K.S. Rifles 1062 Local (Bethune) bombs 59 rifle grenades	
	Issued to Bn Grenade Officer 2 each of Nos 12.3.5.6.9. 12 grenades.	M.M.P

End of Volume XII

27th Division.

(Unit ceased 24.8.15)

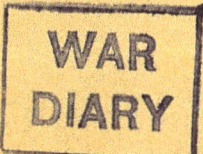

19th INFANTRY BRIGADE AMMUNITION COLUMN.

A U G U S T
(1st to 24th)

1 9 1 5

CONFIDENTIAL

WAR DIARY

of

10th Infantry (Dinside Ammunition Column

From 1st August 24th Aug 1915.

VOLUME XIII

WAR DIARY or **INTELLIGENCE SUMMARY.**

Army Form C. 2118.

Hour, Date, Place	Summary of Events and Information	Remarks and references to Appendices
Nouveau Monde Aug 1st	Returned to 8th Divn Bomb Depot. 45 Red. 33 Blue } rockets 24 white	
Aug 2nd	Rec. from 8 Divn Bomb depot. 9mm 13Bks 1.5" Trench Mortars Issued 20,000 Rds S.A.A. to Cameronians Issued 35 No2, 1 No7 To Bde Grenade Officer. 40 Béthune & 120 209 to 5th Scottish Rifles.	N.P N.P
Aug 3rd	Issued 50 Béthune bombs to A & S.H. 100 Béthune to Bde Grenade Officer, 24 B ettune to R.W.F. 19 rifle grenades 1 No 9 to Cameronians	N.P
Aug 4th	No Bombs or ammunition were issued or received	N.P
Aug 5th	Issued 50 Béthune Gde to 1st Middlesex Regt	N.P
Aug 6th	Capt W.B. ?ook returned from leave & took over command from Lt M.M Pakenham at 1.P.M	
Aug 7th	Nil drawn ??? in Wed	W.J
Aug 8th	Issued 12,000 rds S.A.A , 1 Box mortar amm: 6 Nos 2 to 6 No 6. B 2nd Argyll & S.H. 4000 rds S.A.A 6 No2 & 6 No 6	

Army Form C. 2118.

WAR DIARY
or
INTELLIGENCE SUMMARY.
(Erase heading not required.)

Instructions regarding War Diaries and Intelligence Summaries are contained in F.S. Regs., Part II. and the Staff Manual respectively. Title pages will be prepared in manuscript.

Hour, Date, Place	Summary of Events and Information	Remarks and references to Appendices
LE NOUVEAU MONDE 9th Aug	To 5th S. Rifles, 402 - 6 M.G. - 6 To 2nd R.W.F.	
" 10th Aug	16,000 rds to 2nd A. & S.H.	W.F.
	32,000 rds SAA to 1st Cameronians 16,000 SAA to 5th S. Rifles	
	3000 rds SAA to R.W. Fusiliers	
" 11th Aug	32,000 rds SAA to R.W. Fusiliers	W.F.
" 12th Aug	Received 130 Boxes SAA from 3rd Div R.E. Munro 2 of each type of grenades to R.W. Fusiliers and one of each type to 5th S. Rifles.	W.F.
" 13th Aug	Issued 10 rifle grenades & met + 80 Bethune grenades to 1st Kingsley's. 3000 rds SAA to 5th S. Rifles	W.F.
" 14th Aug	Received 120 Bethune grenades from Bde. Grenade Officer 4000 rds SAA to 5th S. Rifles. Orders received that 14th M.G. Coy would be relieved in night of 15th - 16th - 16th - 17th ed present to billets in neighbourhood of DOULIEU . Then to proceeding to be advised to 2nd Division Amn. Column Division in great with Divisional orders	W.F.

(9/20 6) W 2794 100,000 8/14 H W V Forms/C.2118/11

Army Form C. 2118.

Instructions regarding War Diaries and Intelligence Summaries are contained in F.S. Regs., Part II. and the Staff Manual respectively. Title pages will be prepared in manuscript.

WAR DIARY
or
INTELLIGENCE SUMMARY.
(Erase heading not required.)

Hour, Date, Place	Summary of Events and Information	Remarks and references to Appendices
NOUVEAU MONDE Aug 15ᵗʰ	6pm Orders received to move as Advance Guard to 19ᵗʰ Inf Bde	WJF
Aug 16ᵗʰ	Remained (coy) in rest (two all night pickets posted)	WJF
Aug 17ᵗʰ	Brigade moved during afternoon night orders received for 19ᵗʰ Inf Bde to proceed. Coy to move at 5 am. Trains as per	
Aug 18ᵗʰ	Orders received to proceed to read THEROUANNE	WJF
	9 & 10ᵗʰ Bde's Advance on march to ARDEVILLE then to be detached (1ˢᵗ D, 2ⁿᵈ D)	WJF
Aug 19ᵗʰ	Two days halt at this billet. Farewell message received from Brigadier General Cunliffe 19ᵗʰ July. Brigade to read to Kemp.	WJF
Aug 20ᵗʰ	9 A.M. marched via LA GORGUE — MERVILLE — 50 ST VENANT where Coy and also 3AA were handed over at Ammunition Railhead. Then marched to GUARBECQUE where the Column billeted for the night.	WJF
Aug 21ˢᵗ	8.30 A.M. marched via ISBERGUES — AIRE — MAMETZ	

(9 29 6) W 2794 100,000 8/14 HWV Forms/C. 2118/11

Army Form C. 2118.

WAR DIARY
or
INTELLIGENCE SUMMARY.
(Erase heading not required.)

Instructions regarding War Diaries and Intelligence Summaries are contained in F.S. Regs., Part II. and the Staff Manual respectively. Title pages will be prepared in manuscript.

Hour, Date, Place	Summary of Events and Information	Remarks and references to Appendices
THEROUANNE. Aug 22nd	To THEROUANNE where the Column billeted for the night.	W.T.
FRESSIN Aug 23	Marched at 7 AM via FRUGES - RUISSEAUVILLE to FRESSIN where the Column billeted for the night.	W.T.
LE BOISLE Aug 24	7 AM Marched via WAMIN - HESDIN - REGNAUVILLE to LE BOISLE where the Column billeted for the night.	W.T.
	7 AM Marched via CANCHY to ABBEVILLE when the Column was handed over to Lieut Colonel Trenchant Depot by Capt W.R. Fugold R.S.C.	W.T.
	END of VOLUME XIII	
	End of FINAL VOLUME of WAR DIARY of 19th Infantry Brigade Ammn Column	

www.ingramcontent.com/pod-product-compliance
Lightning Source LLC
Chambersburg PA
CBHW081437160426
43193CB00013B/2304